INDIAN RECIPES

Healthy and Easy to Cook Recipes,cooking for Beginners

(Enjoy This Easy to Follow Collection of Indian Recipes)

Brett Merlino

Published by Alex Howard

© Brett Merlino

All Rights Reserved

Indian Recipes: Healthy and Easy to Cook Recipes,cooking for Beginners (Enjoy This Easy to Follow Collection of Indian Recipes)

ISBN 978-1-77485-019-0

All rights reserved. No part of this guide may be reproduced in any form without permission in writing from the publisher except in the case of brief quotations embodied in critical articles or reviews.

Legal & Disclaimer

The information contained in this book is not designed to replace or take the place of any form of medicine or professional medical advice. The information in this book has been provided for educational and entertainment purposes only.

The information contained in this book has been compiled from sources deemed reliable, and it is accurate to the best of the Author's knowledge; however, the Author cannot guarantee its accuracy and validity and cannot be held liable for any errors or omissions. Changes are periodically made to this book. You must consult your doctor or get professional medical advice before using any of the suggested remedies, techniques, or information in this book.

Table of contents

Part 1 1
KETOGENIC DIET 2
KETOSIS: IS IT HEALTHY? 3
INTERACTION BETWEEN KETOSIS AND DIABETES 4
HOW IS YOUR BODY REACTING TO THIS CHANGE? 5
KETONE BODIES ARE THE FUEL OF BRAIN 9
ADVANTAGES OF KETOSIS 11
SYMPTOMS OF KETO DIET 14
FOODS TO EAT AND AVOID IN CASE OF KETO? 18
CALCULATION METHOD FOR YOUR DAILY MACROS 23
BREAKFAST 26
PANEER METHI CHEESE MARKE CHILLA 26
VEGGIE AND RICOTTA MUFFINS 28
SPICY BACON AND EGG CUPS KETO 30
BREAKFAST BOWL UPMA 32
MEAT AND VEGGIE STUFFED OMELET 34
SNACKS 36
BACON BRUSSELS SPROUTS 36
3.2. CAULIFLOWER TIKKIS 38
3.3. MULTI FILLINGS EGG MUFFINS 40
3.4. CHEESE AND MEAT CHIPS 42
3.5. ROASTED MIXED NUTS 44
3.6. KURKURE PANEER SLICES 46
3.7. CHEESY TAMATAR SALAD 48
3.8. CRUNCHY BROCCOLI TOFU SALAD 50

3.9. SAUSAGE STIR FRY 52
3.10. ZUCCHINI CHEESE AND GARLIC BREADSTICKS 54
3.11. SPINACH YOGURT CHEESE DIP WITH VEGGIES 56
3.12. ZUCCHINI MINI PIZZAS 58
3.13. EGG SALAD IN LETTUCE CUPS 60
3.14. GREEK SALAD WITH FETA 62
3.15. JUGGAD WELE VEGETABLES 64
4. MAINS 66
4.1. JHATPAT JHINGA 66
4.2. FRITTATA WITH VEGETABLES 68
4.3. MASALA FISH FRY 70
4.4. CHINESE STYLE CHICKEN AND BROCCOLI STIR FRY 73
4.5. PALAK PANEER 75
5. STIR FRY 77
5.1. MAST MASALA MUSSELS 77
5.2. KETO CAULIFLOWER EGG FRIED RICE 80
5.3. SOYA PANEER CHEESE KABABS 82
5.4. PALAK METHI ROTI 84
5.5. MUSHROOM PEPPER MASALA 86
5.6. BUTTER GARLIC PRAWNS 88
5.7. TANDOORI CHICKEN BOTI 90
5.8. SAAG MUTTON 92
5.9. GOBHI PARATHAS 94
5.10. KERALA STYLE EGG CURRY 96
6. SIDES 98
6.1. ROASTED LEMONY GARLICKY BROCCOLI 98

6.2. CUCUMBER PEANUT SALAD 101
6.3. GUACAMOLE 103
6.4. MILLIE AUR JULIE WALI SABJI 105
6.5. CHEESE AND CREAM SPINACH 108
7. DESSERTS 110
7.1. KESAR KALAKAND 110
7.2. ALMOND WALNUT CHOCOLATE MOUSSE 112
7.3. COCONUT AND CREAM BARFI 114
7.4. KETO ROCKY ROAD 116
7.5. CHOCOLATE AND COFFEE ICE CREAM 118
7.6. KETO MACAROON 120
7.7. SHRIKHAND 122
7.8. BADAM KULFI 124
7.9. LAUKI KI KHEER 126
7.10. MUG MAIN MASTI 128
Part 2 131
Introduction 132
Chapter 1: Learning the Basics of Indian Cuisine 142
Chapter 02: Common Spices Used in Indian Cuisine and their Properties 160
Chapter 3: Indian Breakfast Recipes 169
Vegetable RavaUpma 169
UpmaSooji with Coconut 171
Puffed Upma Rice 172
Tamarind and RavaUpma Rice 174
RagiRavaIdli 175
RavaIdliSabbakki 177

RavaIdli: Foxtail Millet 178
DosaRava Onion 179
Dosa Buckwheat.. 180
DosaDhaniaPalak.. 181
DosaAval.. 183
DadpePohe... 184
Pohe Tomato with Peas 185
Rotli'sVaghareli 186
The Sesame and Beetroot Thepla.. 189
Dhokla Buckwheat Corn 189
Paneer Crepes and Green Peas**Error! Bookmark not defined.**

Oats Cheela with Paneer Stuffed Palak**Error! Bookmark not defined.**

Chapter 4:Indian Lunch and Dinner Recipes.............**Error! Bookmark not defined.**

Madras Curry Chicken.....**Error! Bookmark not defined.**

Conclusion 192

Part 1

KETOGENIC DIET

Now you have already known about what ketosis is, and there are ways on how you can naturally produce ketones so that you can burn those fats. The keto diet, one of which is utilized that can burn fats and turn them into something beneficial.

This kind of diet can be regarded as high fat. You may even think that this diet is absurd because you are consuming fat to remove excess fat. You will achieve short term weight loss when you start to adhere to the keto diet.

When there are no sugars present in the body, the organs will be looking for other sources of energy in the body. With no carbohydrates, the body is going to use the fat that you have accumulated. The fats are then accumulated into energy. This process happens in the liver, and those fats are converted into a type of acid that we may call as ketones.

The ketones are then delivered to the body and the brain, supplying them with energy. This is one of the diets that use the natural body process to aid weight loss. There have been studies to prove that the ketogenic diet works, especially for obese people.

The ketogenic diet will be offering you two benefits at the same time. You will be burning fats and at the same time gaining energy to supply the body and the brain. Putting the phrase "Hitting two birds with one stone" into action.

KETOSIS: IS IT HEALTHY?

There are people that still questions the credibility of the ketogenic process, although there have been studies or actual people that have done it. If you still doubt this method, then read on because I might change your mind.

The ketogenic diet can even help in making you feel better due to different illnesses such as diabetes, metabolic syndrome, and cardiovascular disease. That is not the only health benefit that you may get with the ketogenic process.

It can also improve the HDL cholesterol level in your body. The HDL cholesterol or the high-density lipoproteins can be considered as good cholesterols.

How Can It Even Help with Different Health Disorders?

In the ketogenic diet, you will be losing excess weight in your body by eating healthier foods. When you eat healthier foods and losing weight at the same time, you are reducing the risk of health conditions. In fact, there are still studies that are ongoing to better understand the beneficial effects of the keto diet to these other health conditions, namely:

o   Cancer
o   Acne
o   Lou Gehrig's Disease
o   Alzheimer's Disease
o   Polycystic Ovary Disease

INTERACTION BETWEEN KETOSIS AND DIABETES

As I've said, ketosis can also be observed with people that have diabetes. Ketosis occurs among patients, not due to the fats but, due to the lack of insulin in their body. If the body lacks insulin, then the glucose cannot be processed.

You can even identify if the diabetes of the patient is not being managed if there are ketones present in their urine.

There are doctors that are using the ketogenic diet as medical measures for patients with type 2 diabetes. Type 2 diabetes can also be identified as non-insulin dependent diabetes. Although the body still produces insulin, it is still not processed well to be used as a source of energy in the body.

This is where the ketogenic diet plays its role, the patients that have type 2 diabetes are advised or recommended to minimize their carbohydrate intake. Carbohydrate is no good for individuals with type 2 diabetes. These carbohydrates are converted into sugar or glucose that can potentially increase the blood sugar level of the patient.

But the ketogenic diet must also be managed, and the ketone levels must be kept stable. High level of ketones can produce a health condition called the ketoacidosis. So keep your level of ketone level up to a stable level only, if you have type 2 diabetes and undergoing the ketogenic diet.

HOW IS YOUR BODY REACTING TO THIS CHANGE?

Now that you already know what ketosis is and it's other aspects, you can now learn about its effect, and how your body can handle it.

We all know that the keto diet, like all other diets, is used to reduce excess weight through the use of fat. But the question is, how does your body handle the ketogenic diet? In general, several things can happen to your body when you undergo the ketogenic diet.

To give you an idea, below are the happenings to your body under ketogenic diet:

- **Weight loss**

Typically the major change that happens to our body due to the ketogenic diet. The ketogenic diet is known to remove excess fat by using those fats to convert them into energy.

- **Keto Flu**

Some people experience the so-called keto flu when they undergo the ketogenic diet. At the first days of your ketogenic diet, you will have this flu due to carbohydrate withdrawal. But the flu is not the only thing that you can experience, and you may also suffer insomnia, headache, and fatigue.

But you don't have to worry or stop the process of the ketogenic diet as the flu, headache, or even fatigue can be fixed. If you start to experience these the things that you have to do is to drink more water and consume more potassium, and you will better in the coming days.

- **Better Brain Function**

It can also benefit the brain. How? You may not know this, but our brain loves fat, and it is a perfect match with the ketogenic diet. The keto diet accumulates or uses the fat that can surely benefit the brain, improving cognitive function. There have been reports that user manifested improvement in their cognitive functions in terms of memory and verbal skills.

We all know that there are vegetable or plants that contain fat. The fat is known as brain food, so you need to inculcate vegetable with fats to improve your cognitive function aside from ingesting drugs or pills.

- **Low Sugar Level**

Through the consumption of food rich in fat, your body is not absorbing carbohydrates or sugar. Without the consumption of carbs and sugar, your sugar level will be increasing at a lower rate. Do you know what does this mean? With low sugar levels, you also have a lower risk of developing diabetes.

This is also good for individuals experiencing blood sugar conditions and type 2 diabetes as their blood sugar level is controlled only at a minimum.

- **Breath Effect**

By the time that you are undergoing the ketogenic diet, your body is adjusting. A certain process in your body may start to happen, and this process is concerned with carbohydrates. The remaining carbohydrates in forms of glycogen will be burned in the liver, thus creating ketones.

These ketones are the fuel of the body and the brain. You are now in ketosis state. How would you know? Try smelling your breath. Does it smell weird? This is one way of identifying if your body has undergone ketosis, through your breath.

This is called the acetone breath, and this happens because of ketosis. The acetone can be considered a manifestation that you are losing weight.

- **Stable Energy Level**

If you are going through weeks under the ketogenic diet, then your body is already adapting. Then your energy level may start to become stable. The continual process of burning fat will happen in your body. Those fats are converted into energy, stabilizing your level, or even increasing it.

The brain will be receiving energy that it needs to function as well as the body. The energy is in the form of ketones that are manufactured in the liver.

- **Core Fat Loss**

Some people do not know that our core contains fat too. This internal fat is called visceral fat. This fat is mostly observed in the areas of the kidneys, liver, and stomach. The ketogenic diet is good to reduce this visceral fat to reduce the risk of having cardiovascular conditions. Conditions such as stroke, heart diseases, and heart attacks may be prevented due to the ketogenic diet.

If you are in the ketogenic diet for weeks now, and you still can't see some physical effect, don't worry. You are already losing those fats in the form of visceral fat. The body may start to burn those inner fat or core fat first, and this is good to reduce your chances of getting those heart diseases and other conditions.

- **Reduced Inflammations**

When you undergo the process of the ketogenic diet, you are also reducing the inflammations in your body. This may be linked with the inner fat. The inner fat and inflammations have risk effects on the body. Both increase the risk of conditions such as cancer and heart diseases.

Through the ketogenic process, the inflammations all over your body are reduced, thus lowering your risk to several conditions. And the keto diet can even protect your brain and improve your other bodily functions because of its energy.

These are the processes that happen in your body when you undergo the ketogenic diet. You may observe changes in your body, but this may seem natural as you are still in the early time of the ketogenic diet.

You may experience a headache or flu. But this is a part of the keto process, and this may be solved if you consume food that is rich in potassium and supplemented with frequent drinking of water.

KETONE BODIES ARE THE FUEL OF BRAIN

The ketones are the acid that is produced by the liver. The ketones are from the fat that the body has accumulated. These are then converted into ketones to fuel the brain to protect it and make it more functional.

The ketones are not only a source of fuel or energy for the brain. It also improves brain or cognitive function, thus, improving your rote memorization skills and your verbal skill in the process.

You should probably be familiar with the term ketogenesis. Ketogenesis refers to the process of producing ketones through the use of fat.

Here's the thing the main source of energy of the brain is usually the sugar or glucose. But when glucose and insulin levels are low, the brain goes to the other source of energy – the ketones produced from the liver by the use of fat or fatty acids.

The ketones can be produced at higher levels if you have undergone a ketogenic diet providing your brain 70% of fuel.

There are also other benefits that the ketogenic diet can provide the brain. It is not only a fuel for the brain, but it can also benefit the user through:

Memory – Some studies proved that individual that has undergone the keto diet manifested improved memory. This can also prevent the risk of Alzheimer's disease and other memory conditions from prevailing.

Brain injury – Some individuals have suffered a brain injury due to accidents and are recovering in hospitals. A ketogenic diet can help quicken their recover because a diet that is low in carbohydrates limits the sugar production of the body.

High level of blood sugar can hinder or slow the recovery process. The ketogenic diet can help the brain to recover at a faster rate while obtaining enough nourishment.

Migraine – Severe migraine are rampant due to several factors; utilization of the keto diet is proven to relieve individual suffering from migraine.

Parkinson's disease – There are also studies conducted that there are individuals who have reported that they felt relief and improvement from the symptoms.

Congenital hyperinsulinism – This is due to hypoglycemia that can potentially lead to brain damage. One way of preventing this is through the process of a ketogenic diet. Some studies have proven that this condition has been successfully treated with the use of the ketogenic diet.

Improve Brain Function – Studies have been conducted that ketogenic diet has improved brain functions.

Not only the ketones are the fuel or energy of the brain, but it can also bring several health benefits concerned with the brain. It can improve cognitive functions and can even relieve you of some brain conditions such as headache, migraine and etc.

ADVANTAGES OF KETOSIS

If you have already made up your mind, and you will be undergoing the ketogenic diet, then you must know the different benefits you may get.

Keto means that you are in the ketogenic diet; therefore, you are undergoing ketosis. Your body is producing ketones to supply your brain with fuel or energy. Below are some of the benefits that you may get under the state of ketosis:

> ### Good for the Heart

If you follow the keto diet through a healthy and stable manner, you are, therefore improving your heart health. If we say a healthy and stable manner, you are eating essential fat from fruits and vegetables and not rely on the pork as a source.

Ketosis can reduce your level of cholesterol, thus reducing your risk from experiencing heart diseases. There are even studies that reported that good cholesterol production has increased due to ketosis or ketogenic diet, and the level of the bad cholesterol was reduced.

> ### Reduce Seizures

Ketosis can also prevent seizures in people that have the condition epilepsy.

> ### Potentially Reduce the Risk of Cancer

Do you know some people that have cancer? How about introducing them to the keto diet? Although you have to get the opinion of the doctor first. But here's the thing ketosis can potentially reduce the risk of cancer from prevailing in your system.

Here how's it work, the keto diet can also be a treatment complementary with the chemotherapy. It can even be connected with the reduction of the blood sugar levels, thus reducing the risk of insulin complications that may be related to cancer.

> **Acne Reduction**

There are numbers of causes that can be associated with the cause of acne. One cause may be associated with blood sugar. If you are that kind of person, who tends to eat food that is high in carbohydrates, you are already putting yourself to the risk of having acne. The carbohydrates can react to with the gut bacteria that could cause blood sugar anomalies.

These anomalies can then influence your skin health. Abnormalities such as sugar fluctuation in the body may cause to spawn acnes. The ketosis promotes fewer carbohydrates in your body, thus already reducing the risk of acne breakouts.

> **Brain Protection**

Ketosis also offers quality protection to the brain. It promotes neuroprotection that can prevent brain conditions from taking over. Ketosis can help cure the dreadful Parkinson's disease, Alzheimer, and even some sleep disorders.

Ketosis also promotes concentration and increased cognitive function in some children. A study has proven.

> **Weight Loss**

Definitely one of the primal benefits of the ketosis. Mainly, this is the cause of why people undergo the ketogenic diet.

The fat in their bodies is converted into ketones, thus reducing excess weights in the body.

SYMPTOMS OF KETO DIET

If there are advantages or benefit of ketosis or ketogenic diet, there is also a side effect. There is always a flaw in the system as they may say. The keto diet also contains a diet that can be minor and can be solved in the process.

To give you an idea on what are the secondary effects of the keto diet, below is the list of the side effects that you may experience in the process of the keto diet.

You shouldn't perform the ketogenic diet for a longer time as it can pose serious conditions and illnesses. These are some conditions that you may develop if an individual chooses to perform the keto diet on longer periods.

o   Kidney Stone formation
o   Acidosis
o   Muscle degeneration

There are also immediate side effects that you may experience once you started on the keto diet. You are experiencing these side effects because your body is still adapting.

- **Keto Flu**

A typical side effect that all dieters experience from the keto diet. When your body is low in carbohydrates, it resorts to the burning of fats as energy and your body is in ketosis. Once your body is in ketosis, you will start to feel several symptoms of the flu such as constipation, vomiting, headache, irritability, and nausea.

All of which is normal due to the change in process in your body. From using sugar, the body will now use the fat in your body. The flu will only last about a week or less than.

- **Sluggishness**

When you are in ketosis, you cease to intake carbohydrates in your body that may result in sluggishness. Your body is still adapting, so typically this is normal and can easily be solved through frequent drinking of water and food that have potassium.

Given that your body has already adapted, you will never feel sluggishness again.

- **Low Blood Sugar Level**

Given that you are eating food rich in fat and not in glucose, your body will inevitably reach a low level of blood sugar. Although this is good because it prevents the risk of diabetes, low blood sugar level can also pose minor problems in the body.

- **Bad Breath**

Once you are in ketosis, you will release this acetone smell in your breathe. This is one manifestation that you are already in ketosis and that you are already losing weight, although your breath would not smell good for a while.

- **Depleted Salt Level**

This happens when you are in the early stages of the keto diet. The body is using the glycogen, which is then stored sugar. Upon usage of this stored sugar, water is released into the blood and out of the body through urine.

When the fluids are released, the salt level can also be depleted. When you develop into ketosis, you are constantly losing salt in your body. Loss of salt in the bed can transpire into symptoms such as headaches or wooziness.

Keep yourself hydrated as you will lose fluids in the process of ketosis, drink water frequently. You can also increase your salt level by drinking soup or broths.

- **Bowel Habit**

Constipation will also occur in your body once you undergo the ketogenic diet. This is due to the change in diet. When the diet is altered, it will take time for body processes to adapt. The gut bacteria will also take time to adapt for it to handle the food that you are eating.

Your habit will be improving within a week, and constipation may not occur. In line with this, keep on drinking water as bowel can affect your fluids. You must keep your fluid level stable by frequently drinking water. You must also take into place eating food that is rich in fiber, nuts, seeds, and legumes. These are the food that has low-carbohydrate content but contains a good source of fiber.

- **Cramps**

Prevailing in the keto diet is loss of salt, and a lower level of salt can cause cramps in your legs. If you have a low salt level in your blood, then you are prone to hyponatremia.

This can be remedied through the same measure. Drink water frequently, and also it is possible to add salt in your food to increase your salt level.

FOODS TO EAT AND AVOID IN CASE OF KETO?

There is food that you have to avoid while you are on the keto diet. To guide you, below are the list of the foods that you can eat while you are on a ketogenic diet. Also, all the food that you want to avoid while you are still in the keto diet.

What to Eat:

- **Seafood**

Seafood is keto dieter's food to go. Fishes such as salmon are very rich in vitamin B, selenium and potassium, and they are free of carbohydrates. So definitely, these food are keto-friendly food.

The shellfish, on the other hand, contains a low amount of carbohydrates, but they can still be included in the ketogenic diet.

- **Vegetables**

To be exact, you should eat vegetables that are low in carbohydrates. Vegetables such as starchy vegetables, that contain low amounts of carbohydrates and calories but very high in nutrients such as vitamin C and other minerals would definitely benefit a keto dieter.

Other vegetables such as broccoli, cauliflower, and other cruciferous vegetables can also be thrown into the diet. They have been connected to food that can lower the risk of cancer and heart diseases.

- **Cheese**

These are the type of food that can be obtained in several places. There are a number of types of cheese that is present in the market but having the same property, low in carbohydrates, thus making them a great food in the ketogenic diet.

Cheese also contains a high amount of saturated fat but can also help reduce the risk of heart disease. It also contains another type of fat that goes by the name of conjugated linoleic acid, which is linked to better development of body composition and fat loss.

- **Avocados**

The avocado is high in nutrients and contains a low amount of carbs. The nutrients that the avocado contains are in the form of potassium. And the potassium can help make the body adapt to a ketogenic diet smoothly.

There has been a study where there are individuals who have eaten avocado have experienced reduced levels of bad cholesterol, and increased level of good cholesterol in their body.

- **Meat and Poultry**

You can also throw into your plate meat and poultry. This is even considered as the staple food of keto dieters because of its protein content. Typically these foods contain no carbohydrates and are highly rich in several vitamins such as vitamin B, potassium, zinc, and selenium.

Grass-fed meat is more advisable to eat because it contains huge amounts of omega-3 fats, antioxidants, and conjugated linoleic acid.

- **Eggs**

Considered as one of the versatile food in the world. An egg will probably contain 1 gram or less carbohydrate, making it a keto-friendly food. Eggs also trigger the release of a hormone that can bring a feeling of fullness. It also helps regulate the level of blood sugar, keeping it stable.

Most of the nutrient in the egg is found in the yolk, but it is advisable to eat all of it so you can reap its full benefit. The nutrients in the yolk are zeaxanthin and lutein.

<u>Here are some of the food that you can eat while on a keto diet: (Categorized)</u>

- **Fat and Oils** - Coconut oil, avocado oil, ghee, olive oil, butter, lard, and mayonnaise.

- **Meat** - Steak, pork, chicken, turkey, ham, sausage, ground beef, and bacon.

- **High-Fat Dairy** - Cheese (either soft or hard), sour cream, cream cheese, and heavy cream.

- **Vegetables** - Olives, cabbage, cauliflower, broccoli, avocado, peppers, zucchini, eggplants, tomatoes, asparagus, cucumber, onion, mushroom, spinach, lettuce, and green beans.

- **Nuts** - Peanuts, almonds, walnuts, hazelnuts, pecans, peanut butter, almond butter, and macadamia nuts.

- **Berries** - Blueberries, Raspberries, and Blackberries.

- **Seafood** - Trout, salmon, cod, catfish, oysters, clams, tuna, halibut, lobsters, crab, mussels, scallops, and snapper.

- **Artificial sweeteners (Sparingly)** - Sucralose and stevia.

- **Alcohol (Sparingly)** - Dry wine, hard liquor, and champagne.

- **Spices**

- **Unsweetened tea or coffee**

What to Avoid:

Here are some of the food that you should avoid while you are on a keto diet.

- **Fruit such as:** Grapefruits, bananas, apples, grapes, oranges, melon, pineapple, cherries, pears, lime, peaches, watermelon, and plum.

- **Root vegetables such as:** Potatoes, sweet potatoes, yucca, turnips, beets, carrots, yams, and carrots.

- **Sweeteners such as:** Sugar cane, honey, maple syrup, corn syrup, aspartame, agave nectar, Splenda, and saccharin.

- **Sweets such as:** Chocolates, candy, pudding, cookies, ice cream, pies, pastries, tarts, buns, cakes, and custards.

- **Alcohol such as:** Beer, wine, cider, and sweetened alcoholic beverages.

- **Sweetened Drinks such as:** Soda, smoothies, juices, coffee, and sweetened tea.

- **Sweetened sauces such as:** Catsup, tomato sauce, salad dressings, hot sauces, and barbecue sauce.

- **Low-fat dairy products such as:** Skim mozzarella, skim milk, fat-free yogurt, and cream cheese.

- **Grain products such as:** Bread, cereal, pasta, rice, oatmeal, corn, pizza, crackers, flour, bagels, popcorn, granola, and muesli.

- **Grains and Starches such as:** Buckwheat, sprouted grains, amaranth, bulgur, quinoa, barley, millet, corn, wheat, rye, rice, and oats.

- **Legumes such as:** Chickpeas, navy beans, lentils, peas, soybeans, black beans, kidney beans, and pinto beans.

- **Some Oils such as:** Soybean oil, canola oil, sunflower oil, sesame oil, grapeseed oil, and peanut oil.

So these are the kind of foods that you can eat while you are still in the keto diet. Below it is some of the food that you must avoid until you have done the keto diet. You have to take into consideration the food that you are eating.

You have to remember that you are still in the keto diet, so you have to manage your food intake. You can use the list above to control the food you eat. To make it more active, create a list that you can put onto your refrigerator.

Contained in that paper are the foods that you can and can't eat. This will serve as your reminder on the different food that you should be eating. Trust me, and this method can help you.

CALCULATION METHOD FOR YOUR DAILY MACROS

If you are on a keto diet, then you should be on a stable consumption of macronutrients per day. There are recommendations that you can follow to supplement your keto diet.

You have to take in mind that you should eat fewer carbohydrates and consume more fat. Generally talking the percentage of the ratio of macronutrients is different within these ranges:

- 15 – 30 percent of calories from protein
- 60 – 75 percent of calories from fat
- 5 – 10 percent of calories from carbs.

It is possible not to count the percentage of the calories, but if you are experiencing difficulty in losing weight, you might as well concern yourself with the calories in your bodies.

If you want to compute for your daily macronutrients intake, there are several sites on the internet that you can use to compute it.

The percentage of fat will be automatically computed, and you have to input some essential details, after that they will be giving you the daily macros that you need to fulfill.

If you want to undergo the keto diet, then you should follow read this because this will provide you information to what ketosis will bring you. There are measures that you have taken into mind before you undergo the process of the keto diet.

This is truly handy because before you dive into the ketogenic processes, you will already be knowledgeable on the do's and don'ts in the keto diet. This will also be your guide as you make your way into the keto diet and until you have reached the end.

Once you have reached this part, your keto experience will be a great success!

BREAKFAST

PANEER METHI CHEESE MARKE CHILLA

Are you looking for a refreshing snack that you can enjoy during the rainy season? This recipe is a light, but the savory version of the paneermethi served in restaurants. One of the best things about this recipe is that it is easy and quick to make. It is also a great alternative to the usual paneer dishes you see or order in restaurants. If you love methi, you should try this recipe. You can serve this dish with naan, roti or plain parantha.It is perfect for those who want to enjoy a flavorful and healthy snack at home.

Cooking time: 20 minutes
Servings: 2

Ingredients:
- 7 oz paneer, cubed
- ½ onion, chopped
- 1 tomato, chopped
- ½ green chilli, chopped
- 1 garlic clove
- ½ teaspoon ginger paste
- 3 tablespoons heavy whipping cream
- 1 tablespoon butter
- 1/2 teaspoon cumin seeds
- 1 ½ teaspoon red chilli powder
- ½ teaspoon coriander powder
- 1 teaspoon turmeric powder
- 1 teaspoon garam masala
- ½ teaspoon dried kasurimethi leaves
- Fresh cilantro leaves, chopped, for serving
- Salt, to taste

Instructions:
1. Season paneer with 1/2 teaspoon turmeric powder, salt and ½ teaspoon red chilli powder.

2. Preheat about 1 tablespoon butter in a skillet. Add paneer and cook for 2-3 minutes per side.

3. Preheat butter in a sauce pan, add cumin, ginger paste, green chilli, onions, garlic, tomato and cook for 2-3 minutes. Let cool and transfer the mixture to a blender, process until of a paste consistency.

4. Return the paste to the pan. Add turmeric powder, red chilli powder, coriander powder, garam masala and cook for 3-4 minutes.

5. Reduce the heat to low and add heavy whipping cream, stir well. Add cooked paneer, Kasurimethi leaves and simmer for 4-5 minutes.

6. Serve topped with cilantro and serve.

Nutritional info (per serving):
482 calories
44.2 g fat
10 g carbohydrate
15.1 g protein

VEGGIE AND RICOTTA MUFFINS

Can't get your child to get veggies? These veggie and ricotta muffins might be the solution you are looking for in this dilemma! These muffins are not just appetizing to look at, but also delicious and healthy. Ricotta is a good source of selenium, phosphorus, calcium, and other essential minerals. Since these muffins are also made with different vegetables, you are assured that your child is eating healthy and yummy foods. These veggie and ricotta muffins are lunch box friendly as well. These savory goodies make a great snack, lunch, or breakfast for both kids and adults.

Cooking time: 30minutes
Servings: 2

Ingredients:
- 2 cups full fat Ricotta Cheese
- 4 eggs
- 4 slices bacon, cooked and crumbled
- 1 tablespoon sundried tomato in olive oil, chopped
- 4 medium mushrooms, chopped
- 1 tablespoon fresh basil, chopped
- ¼ teaspoon onion salt
- ¼ teaspoon garlic opt, chopped
- ¼ cup parmesan, shredded
- ½ teaspoon Italian seasoning

Instructions:
1. Preheat the oven to 400 F.

2. Spray muffin pan with cooking spray.

3. Mix all the ingredients in a bowl until well combined. Divide the batter among cups and bake for 25-30 minutes.

4. Let rest for couple of minutes before serving.

Nutritional info (per serving):
118 calories
8.3 g fat
3.2 g carbohydrate
7.4 g protein

SPICY BACON AND EGG CUPS KETO

Perhaps your love bacon and eggs? Why don't you add some twist to these breakfast favorites? Why not add a bit of spiciness to your dish? This recipe is easy to make. You will have several cups of spicy bacon and egg in no time at all. Imagine waking up on a busy school morning. You want to be able to whip up something easy and quick to make, so you can drop off your kids at school and go to work as soon as possible. Is it going to be spicy? Well, it depends on you. Feel free to adjust the level of spiciness as you see fit.

Cooking time: 30 minutes
Servings: 2

Ingredients:

- 4 oz cheddar cheese, shredded
- 3 oz cream cheese
- 4 chili peppers, de-seeded and sliced
- 12 strips bacon
- 8 eggs, beaten
- ½ teaspoon garlic powder
- ½ teaspoon onion powder
- Salt and pepper, to taste

Instructions:
1. Preheat the oven to 375F. Preheat a non stick skillet over medium heat. Add bacon and cook until slightly browned. Transfer to a plate.

2. Mix cream cheese, eggs, garlic powder, onion powder, salt and pepper in a bowl.

3. Prepare muffin tins and grease with cooking spray.

4. Par-cook bacon so it's semi crisp but still pliable. Save bacon grease to add to mixture.

5. Use a hand mixer, to mix all the other ingredients (except cheddar and 1 jalapeno) together.

6. Grease wells of muffin tin, then place cooked bacon around the edges. Pour the egg mixture into the muffin cups.

7. Top with cheddar cheese and chili pepper ring. Cook for 20-25 minutes. Let cool before serving.

Nutritional info (per serving):
157 calories
12.2 g fat
3 g carbohydrate
10 g protein

BREAKFAST BOWL UPMA

Breakfast is an essential meal of the day, so don't go outside without treating yourself to a healthy and delicious meal first. Make an energy-filled breakfast bowl to start your day right. You can make a breakfast bowl of blended spinach and avocado topped with seeds and fresh fruits. What about guacamole for your breakfast? You can also make a Raspberry Breakfast Bowl. Love vegetables? Why don't you try making your own miso veggie breakfast bowl? With these breakfast bowl recipes, you will find yourself more content and focused throughout the day. These recipes are easy and quick to prepare.

Cooking time: 15 minutes
Servings: 2

Ingredients:

- 7 oz cauliflower
- 2 tablespoons ghee
- 1 teaspoon ginger
- ½ onion
- 4 curry leaves
- 1 tablespoon cumin seeds
- 1 tablespoon mustard seeds
- 1 green chilly, chopped
- Chopped coriander, for serving
- Salt, to taste

Instructions:
1. Add cauliflower florets to a food processor and blend to get rice consistency.

2. Preheat ghee in a deep skillet over medium heat. Add cumin and mustard seeds. Add onion, curry leaves,

ginger and chilli, season with salt. Cook for about 3-4 minutes.

3. Add cauliflower rice and cook for 2 minutes. Add 1 cup water and cover the skillet, cook for 10 minutes, stirring from time to time.

4. Serve topped with coriander.

Nutritional info (per serving):
223 calories
20 g fat
9 g carbohydrate
5 g protein

MEAT AND VEGGIE STUFFED OMELET

You love meat and veggies. Why don't you make meat and veggie stuffed omelet for breakfast? Perhaps you want an egg dish. This meat and veggie stuffed omelet is a light dish that you can eat anytime. It will take you about 15 minutes to prepare. It's that easy. You can teach your kids how to make this dish as well. This is an excellent chance to bond with them. You can double the ingredients to make 2 omelets. Just put the first omelet on a warm plate to keep it well...warm! Top the omelet with hot sauce for added flavor.

Cooking time: 5 minutes
Servings: 2

Ingredients:
- 4 eggs
- 1 cup cooked chicken meat
- 1 cup frozen vegetables mix
- ¼ teaspoon salt
- ¼ teaspoon red chili powder
- 1 green chili, chopped
- ½ onion, chopped
- 1 teaspoon coriander
- 1 tablespoon butter
- A pinch of turmeric

Instructions:
1. Beat eggs, salt, chilli powder, turmeric, coriander, onion and green chilli in a bowl.

2. Preheat butter in a skillet over medium heat. Add chicken and frozen vegetables, cook for about 3-4 minutes.

3. Add the beaten egg mixture, fry the eggs until set on one side. Fold the eggs and cook for about 2-3 minutes more. Enjoy!

Nutritional info (per serving):
255 calories
22 g fat
2 g carbohydrate
13 g protein

SNACKS

BACON BRUSSELS SPROUTS

This recipe is an excellent addition to your dinner table. It doesn't take a lot of time to prepare this dish. The ingredients are also very easy to get. Moreover, this dish is deliciously healthy. The Brussel sprouts soak up the bacon, garlic and olive oil to create an amazing flavor. The bacon complements the Brussel sprouts well. The addition of garlic elevates the flavor and aroma. Don't forget to toss the ingredients a few times throughout the cooking process to prevent them from burning and cooking evenly. If you have leftovers, you can transfer it to a glass jar and store it in the fridge.

Cooking time: 15 minutes
Servings: 4

Ingredients:
- 12 oz Brussels sprouts
- 4 slices bacon, chopped
- 2 garlic cloves
- 1 teaspoon paprika
- 1 tablespoon olive oil
- 1 teaspoon salt
- 1/2 teaspoon pepper

Instructions:
1. Preheat a non stick skillet over medium heat. Add bacon and cook until slightly browned. Transfer to a plate.

2. Add olive oil to the skillet, add sprouts, salt, pepper and paprika. Cook for about 5 minutes. Add garlic and cook for 5 minutes more.

3. Add bacon to the skillet and cook for 1 minute. Serve.

Nutritional info (per serving):
123 calories
8.1 g fat

4 g carbohydrate
7 g protein

3.2. CAULIFLOWER TIKKIS

Are you craving for a healthy and yummy snack that you can serve to your family? Tikkis are usually made by combining mashed potatoes with different ingredients. This recipe uses cauliflower to add vitamins, antioxidants, and fiber to this snack. The spices also impart a wonderful flavor and aroma to the cauliflower tikkis. You can serve this snack to your kids to get them to eat veggies. Cauliflower tikkis can be eaten anytime. You can eat them for your evening snack or even for your breakfast. This recipe is cooked with minimal oil to reduce calorie count and loss of nutrients.

Cooking time: 15 minutes
Servings: 4

Ingredients:
- 8 cauliflower florets
- 1 onion, chopped
- 1/4 cup coriander leaves, chopped
- 2 green chilies, chopped
- 3 tablespoons gram flour
- 1 tablespoons coriander powder
- 1 teaspoon cumin powder
- 1/2 teaspoon black pepper
- 1/2 teaspoon turmeric powder
- 1 teaspoon red chili powder
- 4 tablespoons mustard oil
- Salt, to taste

Instructions:
1. Bring a pan of water to a boil and add salt. Add cauliflower and simmer for 5-6 minutes. Drain and grate the florets to flour texture.

2. Add cauliflower, onion, coriander, green chilies, flour, coriander, cumin, turmeric, chili powder, salt and pepper to a bowl and mix well to combine.

3. Preheat oil in a skillet over medium heat. Shape the mixture into patties and fry in the skillet and fry until browned on both sides.

Nutritional info (per serving):
112 calories
6.6 g fat
4 g carbohydrate
6 g protein

3.3. MULTI FILLINGS EGG MUFFINS

This recipe is an easy grab for hectic mornings. These multi fillings egg muffins are low in carbs and high protein. If you are tired of the same egg dishes, you should try making this recipe today. Shake up your routine and whip up fun egg muffins for your breakfast. These muffins are made with beaten eggs, cheese, seasonings, and other ingredients. Mix everything and pour the mixture into muffin tins. Bake the mixture until set. You can eat these muffins as is or top it with herbs and diced tomatoes. If you're feeding a large crowd, you only need to double the ingredients.

Cooking time: 25 minutes
Servings: 6

Ingredients:
- 12 eggs
- 2 scallions, chopped
- 5 oz chorizo, cooked
- 6 oz cheese, shredded
- 2 tablespoons red pesto
- Salt and pepper, to taste

Instructions:
1. Preheat the oven to 350°F. Prepare muffin tin and grease with cooking spray.

2. Mix all the batter ingredients in a bowl and divide among muffin cups.

3. Bake for 15-20 minutes.

Nutritional info (per serving):
336 calories
26 g fat
2 g carbohydrate
23 g protein

3.4. CHEESE AND MEAT CHIPS

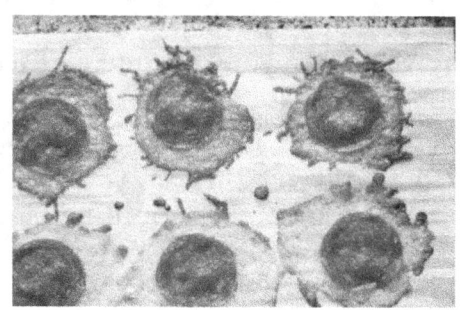

Maybe you love watching movies while munching on some snacks. If you're tired of eating popcorn every time you watch a movie, you can prepare a plate of cheese and meat chips to satisfy your cravings. Follow this recipe for a perfectly delicious snack every time. What's good about this recipe? It is very easy to make, and you can enjoy chips with delicious toppings. You don't have to settle with the same old snacks when you want to satisfy your cravings. Try this recipe! You can bake the cheese and meat in the oven to achieve a perfect gooey and crunchy snack.

Cooking time: 10 minutes
Servings: 4

Ingredients:
- 3 oz salami, 20 slices
- 4 oz parmesan cheese, grated
- 1 teaspoon paprika powder

Instructions:
1. Preheat the oven to 450°F. Prepare a baking sheet and line it with parchment paper.

2. Place the salami slices on the baking sheet. Add the shredded cheese on top of each slice, sprinkle with paprika powder.

3. Bake until the cheese turns golden brown. Serve.

Nutritional info (per serving):
203 calories
15 g fat
3 g carbohydrate
15 g protein

3.5. ROASTED MIXED NUTS

Perhaps some of your friends showed up at your home without any prior notice. Maybe you are throwing a party, and you want your guests to enjoy good food. If you want a snack that is not sweet, you should make your version of roasted mixed nuts. You don't have to settle with the overly salty mixed nuts you can buy at supermarkets or local stores. Freshly roasted mixed nuts are perfect for those who want a healthy snack. The nuts are lightly seasoned with spices and herbs, so expect to get a yummy and fragrant snack. You will get perfectly roasted nuts with no burned spots.

Cooking time: 5 minutes
Servings: 16

Ingredients:
- 3 cups raw nuts (cashews, almonds and Brazil nuts)
- 1 teaspoon sea salt
- 1 tablespoon cinnamon
- 1 teaspoon vanilla essence
- 1 cup granulated Erythritol
- 1/4 cup water

Instructions:
1. Preheat a deep pot over medium heat. Add Erythritol, sea salt, cinnamon and water and mix to combine. Heat up, stirring occasionally.

2. Add the nuts and mix to combine. Cook for about 2-3 minutes, stirring often.

3. Let rest for 1-2 minutes before serving.

Nutritional info (per serving):
135 calories
15 g fat
3 g carbohydrate
4 g protein

3.6. KURKURE PANEER SLICES

Whether you are on a Keto diet or you are following a low carb diet, you will enjoy this recipe. Kurkurepaneer slices are made with cottage cheese marinated in spice powders such as cumin and then deep fried till golden brown. Cottage cheese is rich in protein, which helps prevent sudden declines and hikes in blood sugar level. It also contains calcium, which is required for healthy teeth, heart muscle, and bones. Kurkurepaneer slices are a nice appetizer during small gatherings. Children will also love this dish especially when serving the slices with a cocktail sauce.

Cooking time: 5 minutes
Servings: 8

Ingredients:
- 3 ½ ozpaneer, sliced
- 3 tablespoons breadcrumbs
- 2 tablespoons ground flaxseeds
- 1 teaspoon turmeric powder
- 2 teaspoons red chili powder
- 1 teaspoon cumin powder
- 1 teaspoon garam masala
- 1 teaspoon chat masala
- Salt, to taste
- Oil, for frying

Instructions:
1. Toss paneer in 2 teaspoons corn flour and salt.

2. Mix flaxseeds, turmeric powder, red chilli powder, cumin powder, garam masala and salt in a bowl.

3. Add water and mix well until lump free batter is formed.

4. Preheat oil in a pan, dip each paneer slice into batter and then dip into breadcrumbs. Fry until brown on all sides.

Nutritional info (per serving):
236 calories
11.2 g fat
5.4 g carbohydrate
9.1 g protein

3.7. CHEESY TAMATAR SALAD

Cheesy Tamatar Salad is a quick and easy dish that you can prepare anytime. It's just seasoned tomatoes, olive oil, and fresh mozzarella cheese. Since it only has 3 ingredients, you have to pay attention to the quality of ingredients. Tomatoes that are sweet and plump are the perfect choice for this dish. It becomes more flavorful and sweeter when seasoned with salt. You have to make sure that the mozzarella cheese is fresh. You can also add some balsamic vinegar to the dish. Other options include fresh herbs such as chives, basil, or mint. You can double the number of ingredients to feed a larger crowd.

Cooking time: 5 minutes
Servings: 2

Ingredients:
- 1 cucumber, chopped
- 1 plum tomato, chopped
- 1 red onion, sliced
- 1 lime, juiced
- 3 oz paneer, cubed
- 2 green chillies
- 1 teaspoon chat masala
- Fresh chopped coriander

Instructions:
1. Mix cucumber, tomato, onion and paneer in a bowl.

2. Add coriander and sprinkle with lime juice, toss to coat.

3. Add chat masala and stir to combine. Serve.

Nutritional info (per serving):
152 calories
4.5 g fat
5.3 g carbohydrate

5.7 g protein

3.8. CRUNCHY BROCCOLI TOFU SALAD

Crunchy Broccoli Tofu Salad is delicious and satisfying. You can put the salad together when you are prepping your meals for the week. Perhaps you want to get more vegetables in your diet. Maybe you don't order salads at restaurants because you're afraid that they will be bland. This salad is perfect for those who love crispy tofu and broccoli. You can store the topper, mix-ins, and salad base in the fridge for 3 to 5 days or longer. You can adjust the number of ingredients to create enough salad for dinner or pack up for one week's worth of salad.

Cooking time: 15 minutes
Servings: 4

Ingredients:

- 1 (14 oz) package extra-firm tofu
- 1 head of broccoli, florets chopped
- 2 tablespoons vegetable oil
- 2 scallions, sliced
- 1 hot chili, sliced
- Salt and pepper, to taste

For the Dressing:
- 1 tablespoon rice vinegar
- ½ teaspoon soy sauce
- ¼ teaspoon sugar
- 2 tablespoons sesame oil
- 2 teaspoons sesame seeds, toasted

Instructions:
1. Preheat the oven to 400 F. Toss broccoli florets with 1 tablespoon vegetable oil, salt and pepper. Place on a baking sheet and bake for about 5 minutes, remove from the oven. Reduce oven heat to 350 F.

2. Preheat the remaining oil in a pan. Add tofu and sprinkle with salt and pepper. Add to the pan and cook for about 1-2 minutes per all sides.

3. Transfer to the baking sheet and cook for 8-10 minutes.

4. Mix all dressing ingredients in a bowl. Mix broccoli, tofu, scallions and chili, top with dressing, toss to coat. Serve.

Nutritional info (per serving):
238 calories
20.2 g fat
5.8 g carbohydrate
11.1 g protein

3.9. SAUSAGE STIR FRY

Sausage Stir Fry is a healthy meal that you won't feel guilty serving to your family. It's made with a load of veggies and quality sausage cooked in very hot oil. One of the best things about this dish is that the vegetables look vibrant but remain crisp-tender. Mix an all-natural sausage, and you will have a delicious meal bursting with flavor and aroma. This recipe is very easy to make. You only need to slice up the onion, sausage, and sweet bell peppers and stir fry the mix. This recipe is a crowd-pleaser and won't take up too much of your time to prepare.

Cooking time: 25 minutes
Servings: 4

Ingredients:
- 10 chicken sausages, sliced
- 2 tablespoons oil
- 1 tablespoon butter
- 10 garlic cloves, crushed
- 2 onions, sliced
- 1 bell pepper, sliced
- 2 teaspoons red chili pepper
- 1 teaspoon garam masala
- 1 teaspoon pepper powder
- 1 teaspoon vinegar
- ½ cup tomato ketchup
- Salt, to taste

Instructions:
1. Preheat oil and butter in a pan. Add crushed garlic and cook for about 1 minute.

2. Add onions and salt. Cook until browned. Add sausage and cook for 8-10 minutes.

3. Add peppers and sauté for 2-3 minutes. Add chili powder and stir well.

4. Add ketchup and toss to coat. Add vinegar, garam masala powder and pepper powder, mix well to combine. Serve.

Nutritional info (per serving):
345 calories
12 g fat
4 g carbohydrate
15 g protein

3.10. ZUCCHINI CHEESE AND GARLIC BREADSTICKS

Transform zucchini into bread with this recipe. Are you looking for a keto-friendly and low-carb substitute to traditional breadsticks? The recipe has a thin, pizza-like crust, topped with melted cheese with a really chewy crust. These cheesy breadsticks are a low-carb option to take-out cheesy bread. Each serving is oozing with parmesan and mozzarella. Since you're making a keto-friendly snack, you can replace cornstarch with almond flour. You will also get some extra veggies when you make these breadsticks. This recipe is also easy and quick to prepare. Your kids will love these breadsticks, so it's time to whip up some!

Cooking time: 40 minutes
Servings: 2

Ingredients:
- 4 zucchinis, grated
- ⅓ cup parmesan cheese, grated
- ⅓ cup cheddar cheese, grated
- ½ cup mozzarella cheese, grated
- 1 egg
- 1 tablespoon garlic powder
- 1 teaspoon pepper
- ½ teaspoon red pepper flakes
- ½ teaspoon salt

Instructions:
1. Preheat the oven to 400ºF.

2. Mix grated zucchini, parmesan cheese, garlic powder, pepper, red pepper flakes, salt, and egg in a bowl. Mix well to combine.

3. Line the baking sheet with parchment paper. Spread the mixture evenly on the baking sheet, about ½ inch thick.

4. Bake for 35-40 minutes. Top with cheddar and mozzarella cheese. Bake for 10 minutes more.

5. Let cool and slice into sticks. Serve.

Nutritional info (per serving):
383 calories
23 g fat
10 g carbohydrate
28 g protein

3.11. SPINACH YOGURT CHEESE DIP WITH VEGGIES

Are you looking for a luscious dip that you can bring to a picnic? Whip up this spinach yogurt cheese dip with veggies and enjoy it as part of a healthy snack or side. Since it uses Greek yogurt, expect this dip to be delicious and creamy. The best thing about this spinach yogurt cheese dip is that it has more protein and less fat than the usual dips. You can prepare it in just a few minutes. Combine all ingredients, and you will get that creamy, cheesy goodness everyone will love. You can store it in the fridge for 2 days. Just reheat the dip before serving.

Cooking time: 2 minutes

Servings: 8

Ingredients:
- 2 cups fresh spinach
- 8 oz low-fat cream cheese
- 2 tablespoons Greek yogurt
- 3/4 cup cheddar cheese, shredded
- 1/4 cup parmesan cheese, shredded
- 1/4 teaspoon garlic powder
- 1/2 teaspoon salt

Instructions:
1. Add spinach to a skillet and cook over medium heat for 2-3 minutes, stirring frequently.

2. Transfer to a plate and let cool slightly. Chop the spinach.

3. Mix cream cheese and Greek yogurt in a bowl. Add cheddar, parmesan, garlic powder and salt, stir well to combine.

4. Add spinach and stir well. Microwave the dip for 30 seconds and stir well. Serve with sliced veggies of choice.

Nutritional info (per serving):
117 calories
8.8 g fat
3.2 g carbohydrate
6.2 g protein

3.12. ZUCCHINI MINI PIZZAS

Do you love zucchini and pizzas? How about making zucchini mini pizzas at home? Topped with lots of mozzarellas, mini pepperonis, and sauce, zucchini makes a great base for pizza. It's the perfect low carb recipe for those who love pizzas! Zucchini is extremely versatile, flavorful, and healthy. It has zero fat and is loaded with fiber and vitamin B6, K and C. Zucchini Mini Pizzas are easy to put together. Whether it is a party or a sleepover, this recipe will be a hit with everyone. You can top your mini pizzas with low carb veggies or crumbled feta cheese for an extra burst of flavor.

Cooking time: 20 minutes
Servings: 24

Ingredients:
- 1 zucchini, cut into 1/4 inch-slices
- 1/3 cup pizza sauce
- 3/4 cup mozzarella cheese, shredded
- 1/2 cup miniature pepperoni slices
- Minced fresh basil
- Salt, pepper, to taste

Instructions:
1. Preheat broiler. Place zucchini slices in a single layer on a greased baking sheet.

2. Broil for 1-2 minutes per side.

3. Sprinkle zucchini with salt and pepper, top with sauce, cheese and pepperoni. Broil for about 1 minute. Serve topped with basil.

Nutritional info (per serving):
29 calories
2 g fat
1 g carbohydrate
2 g protein

3.13. EGG SALAD IN LETTUCE CUPS

Egg salad in lettuce cups is a simple yet appetizing snack. You can also eat it for lunch. This recipe tucks fresh tomato, bacon, and creamy egg salad into a crisp lettuce leaf. You can add some mustard, hot sauce, or diced pickles for extra flavor. For a delicious and light lunch, you can serve this dish with fresh fruits. This recipe is easy to make, and you can complete it before you leave for work. You can hard boil the eggs as well as cook and chop the bacon in advance. Transfer the bacon to an airtight container and store it in the fridge.

Cooking time: 2 minutes
Servings: 4

Ingredients:
- 4 eggs, hard boiled, sliced
- 1 avocado, diced
- 8 leaves lettuce
- 2 teaspoons lemon juice
- 3 tablespoons mayonnaise
- 2 tablespoons chives, chopped
- 1/2 teaspoons salt
- 1/4 teaspoon pepper

Instructions:
1. Mix lemon juice, mayonnaise, chives, salt and pepper in a bowl.

2. Mix eggs and avocado in a bowl. Top with the dressing and toss well to combine.

3. Add ¼ cup of the mixture into each lettuce leaf and serve.

Nutritional info (per serving):
136 calories
12 g fat
0 g carbohydrate

5 g protein

3.14. GREEK SALAD WITH FETA

Craving for some Greek salad? Try this recipe! This chunky Greek salad with feta is loaded with protein. It's fresh, healthy, and bright! You can enjoy sliced tomatoes, cucumber chunks, crumbled feta and olives in a lemon dressing infused with herbs. Are you having a hard time getting your child to eat veggies? You can use a colorful variety of olives with different sizes to entice your child to eat this salad. Greek salad with feta can be eaten as is or served with grilled fish. You can also serve it with pita chips so that you can enjoy this dish like a sandwich or burrito.

Cooking time: 2 minutes
Servings: 4

Ingredients:
- 1 cucumber, sliced
- 2 bell peppers, sliced
- ½ red onion, sliced
- 4 oz Feta cheese, cubed
- 1/2 cup kalamata olives, pitted
- ¼ cup olive oil
- 1 tablespoon red wine vinegar
- 1 teaspoon dried oregano
- Salt, pepper, to taste

Instructions:
1. Mix all the vegetables in a bowl. Add Feta cheese.

2. Add olives, drizzle with olive oil, vinegar, oregano, salt and pepper. Toss well to coat.

3. Serve right away.

Nutritional info (per serving):
226 calories
20 g fat
6 g carbohydrate

11 g protein

3.15. JUGGAD WELE VEGETABLES

JuggadWele vegetables are packed with vitamins, minerals, fiber, and antioxidants. There are a lot of veggies to choose from, so you will not get bored or tired with this recipe. You can make it for your snack or lunch. This recipe is also easy to prepare. Just make sure to wash the greens properly before cooking them. Don't chop and then wash the veggies. Do the opposite to get maximum nutritional benefits. Don't expose the veggies to air and light after chopping them up. It is best to use veggies immediately. You can serve this dish with fresh fruits.

Cooking time: 20 minutes
Servings: 4

Ingredients:
- 1 head broccoli, cut into florets
- 2 carrots, peeled and chopped
- 2 parsnips, peeled and chopped
- 1 teaspoon ground coriander
- 1 teaspoon turmeric
- 1 teaspoon curry powder
- 1 teaspoon cumin seeds
- 3 tablespoons olive oil
- 1 teaspoon grated ginger
- Sea salt, pepper, to taste

Instructions:
1. Preheat the oven to 450 F.

2. Add all the vegetables to a bowl. Add coriander, turmeric, curry powder, cumin, salt and pepper, toss well to coat.

3. Add oil and toss to coat. Place the vegetables on a baking sheet in one layer. Bake for about 20 minutes. Toss with grated ginger and serve warm.

Nutritional info (per serving):
112 calories
7.3 g fat
1.7 g carbohydrate
11.5 g protein

4.MAINS

4.1.JHATPAT JHINGA

If you love prawns, you shouldn't pass up the chance to cook your own JhatpatJhinga. It's made with prawns, pureed tomatoes and spice powders. This combination brings out the flavor of the prawns. JhatpatJhinga can be eaten with rotis or rice. Here are some tips to observe. Cook the prawns for a few minutes. If you overcook the prawns, they're going to be hard, and they won't be easy to chew. You can boil the prawns in hot water before cooking them. Aside from these precautions, JhatpatJhinga is pretty easy to cook. You can enjoy it with your family afterward.

Cooking time: 20 minutes
Servings: 4

Ingredients:

For Prawns:
- 1 lb prawns without shells
- 1/2 teaspoon turmeric powder
- 1 tablespoon oil
- 1/2 teaspoon salt

For the Gravy:
- 2 ½ cups onions finely chopped
- 2 ½ cups tomatoes finely chopped
- 2 tablespoons tomato paste
- 2 ½ teaspoons chili powder
- 1 teaspoon turmeric powder
- 1 tablespoon ginger garlic paste
- 6 tablespoons oil
- 3 ½ oz spring onions, for serving
- Fresh coriander, for serving
- Salt, taste

Instructions:

1. Preheat oil in a pan over medium heat. Add prawns, salt, turmeric and cook for about 5 minutes. Remove from heat and set aside.

2. Preheat some oil in a separate pan over medium heat. Add onions and cook for about 3-4 minutes. Add ginger garlic paste, cook for 1 minute.

3. Add chili powder, turmeric powder and salt, cook for about 30 seconds.

4. Add tomatoes and cook for about 5 minutes. Add tomato paste to the gravy and cook for 1 minute.

5. Add prawns and cook for about 10 minutes. Add spring onions and coriander, stir well and serve.

Nutritional info (per serving):
349 calories
24.4 g fat
8.9 g carbohydrate
16.1 g protein

4.2. FRITTATA WITH VEGETABLES

This recipe is perfect for lunch and breakfast. It's also great for a light evening meal. Frittata with vegetables is low in carb and easy to make. It is a good way to use leftover herbs, veggies, and cheese. This recipe is similar to a baked omelette that can double as brunch or dinner. It can feed a crowd. One of the best things about this recipe is that you don't really need to go out to shop for the ingredients. You only need to go out when you don't have the ingredients at home. This recipe can be stored in the fridge for up to 3 days.

Cooking time: 30 minutes
Servings: 4

Ingredients:
- 4 bacon slices, diced
- 1 cup mushrooms, sliced
- 2 tablespoons butter
- 4 oz baby spinach
- 1 cup Cheddar cheese, shredded
- 6 eggs
- 1/4 cup heavy cream
- Salt, pepper, to taste

Instructions:
1. Preheat the oven to 355F. Preheat an oven proof pan over medium heat. Add bacon and cook for about 4 minutes. Add butter and mushrooms and cook for about 3 minutes.

2. Add spinach and cook for 2 minutes more. Remove from heat and sprinkle everything with cheese.

3. Mix eggs, cream, salt and pepper in a bowl. Pour the mixture to the pan and bake for 20 minutes.

4. Let rest for 5-10 minutes and serve.

Nutritional info (per serving):
426 calories
36 g fat
3 g carbohydrate
21 g protein

4.3. MASALA FISH FRY

Masala fish fry makes for a great side dish or appetizer. This recipe yields a mouth-watering crispy fish. You have to marinate the fish two times. The first marination allows the fish to absorb all the spice and flavors. The second marination is done to produce a crusty fish. The most important part about this recipe is the fish selection. The fish should be alive and then cut into your desired size and shape. If it's too big, the taste won't be satisfactory even though you followed the instructions. You can serve this dish as a side with jeera rice, coconut rice, or ghee rice.

Cooking time: 40 minutes
Servings: 4

Ingredients:

- 10 fish slices
- 1 tablespoon rice flour
- 10 dry red chillies
- 2 tablespoons coriander seeds
- 10 peppercorns
- 1 teaspoon cumin seeds
- 1 teaspoon fennel seeds
- 2 cloves
- 1 inch cinnamon stick
- 1 onion, chopped
- 2 curry leaves
- 5 garlic cloves
- 1/4 teaspoon turmeric powder
- 1 teaspoon lemon juice
- Salt, to taste
- Oil, for frying

Instructions:

1. Toast roast the red chillies, coriander seeds, peppercorns, cumin seeds, fennel seeds, cloves and cinnamon stick until nice aroma comes out. Set aside.

2. Add few drops of oil to the same pan, add onions, curry leaves and garlic cloves, cook for 3-4 minutes.

3. Add roasted spices and onion-garlic to a jar, add turmeric powder, lemon juice and grind into a fine and thick paste with water.

4. Rub the thick paste evenly over the fish slices and let rest for at least two hours.

5. Fry the fish slices with enough oil over medium heat until browned on all sides. Serve.

Nutritional info (per serving):
314 calories
18.5 g fat
5.8 g carbohydrate
33.4 g protein

4.4. CHINESE STYLE CHICKEN AND BROCCOLI STIR FRY

Desi Chinese Style Chicken and Broccoli Stir Fry is a fusion stir fry dish that is loaded with sweet, spicy and slightly tangy flavors. It is a healthy version of a restaurant favorite that combines chicken, broccoli, ginger and garlic for a scrumptious weeknight dinner. It is fast and easy to make, so it's perfect for those who have a busy schedule. You can prepare it within 30 minutes. You can also toss in any veggies or meat you have. Whether you are a seasoned cook, or you want to try a new dish, your whole family will enjoy this Desi Chinese Style Chicken and Broccoli Stir Fry.

Cooking time: 15 minutes
Servings: 4

Ingredients:
- 1 lb boneless skinless chicken breast, cut into bite sized pieces
- ¼ lb broccoli, cut into small florets
- 1 tablespoon olive oil
- 1/2 onion, minced
- 2 garlic cloves, minced
- 1 tablespoon fresh ginger, minced
- 1 tablespoon low sodium soy sauce
- 1 teaspoon sesame seed oil
- 2 teaspoons rice vinegar
- 2 teaspoons hot sauce

Instructions:
1. Preheat oil in a skillet or a pan over medium heat. Add onions and garlic, cook for 3-4 minutes.

2. Add chicken and ginger, cook for 1 minute more.

3. Add soy sauce, sesame oil, rice wine vinegar and hot sauce. Cook for about 8-10 minutes, stirring from time to time.

4. Add broccoli and 1-2 tablespoons water. Cover the pan and cook for about 1-2 minutes. Serve.

Nutritional info (per serving):
190 calories
6.5 g fat
3.8 g carbohydrate
12 g protein

4.5. PALAK PANEER

Palakpaneer is an Indian dish made with paneer or cottage cheese and pureed or blanched spinach (palak). It is eaten with naan, ghee rice, paratha, roti or plain rice. If you're following a low oxalate diet, you can blanch the spinach. To make palakpaneer, you need to blanch the spinach before making a puree. If you don't like garlic, you can reduce its amount accordingly. You can also decide whether you're going to use tomatoes or not. Always pick tender spinach that's light green. Dark leaves are not tasty. Avoid frozen spinach and the stems and stalks of spinach as it can make the dish bitter.

Cooking time: 30 minutes
Servings: 4

Ingredients:

- 1 cup paneer, cubed
- 4 cups palak (or green spinach)
- 1 onion, chopped
- 1 teaspoon minced garlic
- ½ teaspoon minced ginger
- 1 teaspoon red chilli powder
- 1 teaspoon coriander powder
- ½ teaspoon cumin powder
- ¼ teaspoon turmeric powder
- A pinch kasurimethi
- 1 teaspoon garam masala
- 2 teaspoons ghee
- A pinch hing
- 1 teaspoon tomato paste
- 1 cup milk
- 1 tablespoon plain yogurt

Instructions:

1. Bring a pot of water to a boil and add spinach leaves. Simmer for about 2 minutes and remove from heat. Add to a blender and puree to a smooth paste.

2. Preheat ghee in a pot. Add cumin powder and add the chopped onions. Sauté until golden brown and add coriander powder, turmeric, chilli powder and hing. Cook for a few seconds.

3. Add minced ginger and garlic and the tomato paste. Mix well and add the pureed spinach.

4. Add milk. Mix well, bring to boil and add the kasurimethi and salt.

5. Cook covered for about 6-8 minutes. Slowly add the paneer pieces, stir to coat.

6. Sprinkle with garam masala, mix well and remove from the heat.

7. Serve topped with yogurt.

Nutritional info (per serving):
165 calories
11.4 g fat
7 g carbohydrate
12 g protein

5.STIR FRY

5.1.MAST MASALA MUSSELS

Tomatoes and fennel are often paired with mussels. How about adding a twist to steamed mussels? Garam masala adds a curry flavor to the tender mussels and coconut milk broth. This sumptuous recipe is a real treat for those who love seafood. It combines soft mussels with Indian spices, so you can expect to have a fragrant and delectable dish. This recipe is easy and quick to prepare. You can serve it as a dinner party dish. It doesn't matter whether you're a newbie or a seasoned chef. The ingredients can be purchased easily, and you can cook it in less than an hour.

Cooking time: 20 minutes
Servings: 4

Ingredients:
- 4 lbs mussels, scrubbed
- 1 cup basil leaves, chopped
- 1/4 cup extra-virgin olive oil
- 1 onion, chopped
- 1 fennel bulb, trimmed and chopped
- 4 garlic cloves, chopped
- 1 teaspoon garam masala
- 1/4 teaspoon hot red-pepper flakes
- 1 can (15 oz) diced tomatoes with juices
- 2/3 cup canned unsweetened coconut milk

Instructions:
1. Preheat oil in pot over medium-high heat. Add onion, fennel, garlic, garam masala, red-pepper flakes, salt and pepper, cook for about 10-12 minutes, stirring occasionally.

2. Add tomatoes with juices and coconut milk, bring everything to a boil. Add mussels and cover the pot. Cook for 8 - 10 minutes. Discard unopened mussels after 10 minutes.

3. Add basil, stir well and serve.

Nutritional info (per serving):
625 calories
32.5 g fat
6.9 g carbohydrate
36.2 g protein

5.2. KETO CAULIFLOWER EGG FRIED RICE

You don't need to settle with greasy or sub-par food. With this recipe, you can make your own keto cauliflower egg fried rice at the comfort of your own home. Cooking can be made more fun and simpler. You don't need to prepare a fancy wok to prepare this recipe. The secret to this recipe is the cauliflower. You have to process the cauliflower to achieve the desired rice consistency. After processing the cauliflower, you can throw it in a simple skillet and allow it to crisp up. Add garlic, veggies, onion, soy sauce, and sesame oil and you have your own homemade keto cauliflower egg fried rice!

Cooking time: 10 minutes
Servings: 4

Ingredients:
- 12 oz cauliflower, riced
- 1 oz green onion, sliced
- 1/4 cup carrot, diced optional
- 2 tablespoons butter
- 2 garlic cloves, crushed
- 1 egg, beaten
- 2 tablespoons soy sauce
- 1 teaspoon toasted sesame oil

Instructions:
1. Melt butter in a skillet over medium heat. Add carrots and cauliflower. Cook for about 5 minutes, stirring often.

2. Add green onions, cook for 2-3 minutes. Add garlic and cook for 1 minute more. Add egg and stir well to combine. Cook for 1-2 minutes, stirring frequently.

3. Add soy sauce and sesame oil. Serve.

Nutritional info (per serving):
114 calories

8 g fat
6 g carbohydrate
4 g protein

5.3. SOYA PANEER CHEESE KABABS

Soya paneer cheese kababs can be served as a snack for cold evenings with a cup of warm beverage. You can also serve it as an appetizer during potluck and game nights. If you are expecting guests, you can prepare this dish for them. Soya paneer cheese kababs are loaded with mozzarella cheese, soya chunks, onions, green chili and other spices that will delight your taste buds. You don't have to visit the nearest restaurant to enjoy these kebabs. This dish can be paired with your favorite dip or chutney. You can enjoy these kebabs on your own or share it your family and friends.

Cooking time: 25 minutes
Servings: 6

Ingredients:
- 1 cup soya granules, soaked in hot water for 10 mins, drained
- 1 cup paneer, grated
- 1 cup rice, pressed
- 2 onion, chopped
- 4 green chilli, chopped
- 1 tablespoon ginger paste
- 2 tablespoon chat masala
- 1 tablespoon coriander powder
- 1 tablespoon coriander leaves, chopped
- 1 tablespoon garlic paste
- 2 tablespoon garam masala powder
- 1 tablespoon chilli powder
- 2 cup mozzarella, grated
- 1 1/2 cup refined oil
- Salt, to taste

Instructions:
1. Mix paneer, soya and the remaining ingredients in a bowl.

2. Divide the dough into smaller portions and shape them into kebabs and put onto a thick seekh.

3. Preheat oil in a deep pan over medium heat. Cook kebabs until browned on all sides. Serve.

Nutritional info (per serving):
180 calories
14 g fat
8 g carbohydrate
8 g protein

5.4. PALAK METHI ROTI

Palakmethi roti can be served for breakfast or packed for your child's school lunch box. You have to knead the dough with methi leaves and spinach to make this flatbread. If you want to add greens to your daily meal, you can mix some veggies in the dough such as spinach. You can also add fenugreek seeds to this dish. Fenugreek seeds are rich in dietary fiber, which can help lower blood sugar levels and slow gastric emptying. You can use leftover veggies from your previous meal. You can serve palakmethi roti for breakfast with pickle and curd.

Cooking time: 15 minutes
Servings: 4

Ingredients:

- 1 cup blanched spinach, chopped
- 1/2 cup fenugreek (methi) leaves, chopped
- 2 cups coconut flour
- 1/2 cup paneer cheese, cubed
- 1 teaspoon ghee
- 1 onion , chopped
- 4 garlic cloves, grated
- 3 cardamoms
- 2 cloves
- ½ teaspoon garam masala
- Salt, to taste

Instructions:
1. Preheat ghee in a pan over medium heat. Add cardamoms, cloves, onion and garlic. Cook for 3-4 minutes.

2. Add spinach, fenugreek leaves, paneer, garam masala and salt. Cook for 3-4 minutes, stirring often. Let cool slightly.

3. Mix flour and spinach mixture in a bowl. Slowly add water and knead the mixture into smooth dough.

4. Divide the dough into 8-10 portions of equal size. Roll each portion out into a flat paratha about 6-7 inches in diameter.

5. Preheat a skillet and place the rolled out paratha in the skillet, cook for 1-2 minutes per side. Serve.

Nutritional info (per serving):
169 calories
14 g fat
5 g carbohydrate
8 g protein

5.5. MUSHROOM PEPPER MASALA

Mushroom pepper masala is a spicy side dish popular in Indian restaurants. It's made with button mushroom seasoned with garlic and pepper. Mushrooms are also called vegetarian meat due to its texture. It is rich in protein and contains zero fat. If you are watching your cholesterol level, you can include mushroom in your diet. It is like eating meat. Since mushroom is healthier than meat, you can eat without feeling any guilt. If it is your first time eating a mushroom, you can combine it with your favorite veggies. You will gradually love mushrooms and enjoy eating it as is.

Cooking time: 30 minutes
Servings: 4

Ingredients:

- 1 lb mushroom, chopped
- 1 onion, chopped
- 1 tomato, chopped
- 1 teaspoon ginger garlic paste
- 4 garlic cloves, crushed
- 1 green chilli, chopped
- 1 teaspoon coriander powder
- ½ teaspoon red chili powder
- ¼ teaspoon turmeric powder
- ¼ teaspoon garam masala
- 1 tablespoon olive oil
- ¼ teaspoon mustard seeds
- ¼ teaspoon cumin seeds
- ½ lemon, juiced
- Fresh cilantro, for serving
- Salt, to taste

Instructions:

1. Preheat oil in a pan over medium heat. Add mustard seeds and cumin seeds, cook until soft.

2. Add onions, curry leaves and green chili, cook for 3-4 minutes. Add ginger garlic paste and chopped tomatoes.

3. Add turmeric powder, chili powder, coriander powder and garam masala. Cook for about 5-7 minutes.

4. Add mushrooms and cook it covered with little water, for about 5 minutes. Uncover and cook until all water evaporates.

5. Add lemon juice and stir well. Cook for 1 minute. Serve topped with cilantro.

Nutritional info (per serving):
208 calories
17 g fat
6.1 g carbohydrate
18.4 g protein

5.6. BUTTER GARLIC PRAWNS

Combining butter and garlic in a prawn skillet will make your day, especially if you love seafood. If you are on a diet, you can make this dish on your cheat day. Every juicy bite of the prawn is worth it. The best thing about this dish is that you can prepare it in less than 20 minutes. The method used to make this dish is neat and quick. You need to layer all the ingredients into a clean pot and then leave it on the stove to cook. It's that easy. Enjoy an amazing combination of buttery and garlicky goodness!

Cooking time: 18 minutes
Servings: 4

Ingredients:
- 1 lb shrimp, peeled and deveined
- 6 tablespoons butter
- 5 garlic cloves, minced
- 1/2 cup chicken stock
- ¼ teaspoon red pepper flakes
- 2 tablespoons lemon juice
- 2 tablespoons parsley, minced
- Salt, pepper, to taste

Instructions:
1. Preheat 2 tablespoons butter in a skillet over medium heat. Add shrimp, season with salt and pepper, cook for 4-5 minutes.

2. Transfer shrimp to a plate. Add garlic and cook for about 30 seconds.

3. Add chicken stock and stir well to combine. Cook for about 5-10 minutes.

4. Add the remaining butter, lemon juice and red pepper. Stir well and cook for 2 more minutes.

5. Add shrimp and stir to combine. Serve topped with parsley.

Nutritional info (per serving):
307 calories
20 g fat
3 g carbohydrate
27 g protein

5.7. TANDOORI CHICKEN BOTI

Tandoori chicken boti can be served with roti, naan or bread. You can also serve it with a salad of your choice. One of the best things about this dish is that you can make it without using an oven. If you love chicken, you can bring its flavor to a whole new level by adding the right spices and cooking it perfectly. Use medium-sized veggies and fresh herbs. You can make this dish anytime as well as enjoy it without feeling any guilt. Follow the recipe below and share your Tandoori chicken boti with your family and friends.

Cooking time: 30 minutes
Servings: 8

Ingredients:

- 8 chicken thighs
- 1/2 cup plain yogurt
- 2 tablespoons hot curry paste
- 1 tablespoon fish sauce
- 1 tablespoonlime juice
- 1/2 teaspoon stevia or splenda

Instructions:

1. Combine all the marinade ingredients in a gallon sized ziploc bag and mix well.

2. Rinse and pat dry chicken thighs, and using a sharp knife, make a few deep cuts across the top of each thigh.

3. Put chicken into the ziploc bag, squeeze the excess air out and seal. Squeeze and squish the bag to make sure the chicken is well coated, then toss into the fridge. Marinate for at least 4 hours (overnight is even better).

4. Put chicken on a foil or parchment lined sheet pan.

5. Heat the oven to 450F and bake the chicken for about 40 minutes (longer if larger chicken thighs).

6. Once cooked, it is ready to serve.

Nutritional info (per serving):
531 calories
37 g fat
5 g carbohydrate
33 g protein

5.8. SAAG MUTTON

Mutton complements the spinach in this recipe. Saag mutton is a popular Indian dish that is rich in nutrition and flavor. Spinach combines perfectly with the strong flavor of goat/lamb meat. Saagmuttin is a great weekend recipe that you can eat with rotis or flavored rice. It is a warm and comforting dish that you can serve on rainy days. You can choose to use chopped spinach and slow cook the dish until it's done. Pureed spinach, however, improves the creaminess and richness of the dish. Adding pureed spinach when the meat is almost done keeps the color and flavor of the spinach fresh.

Cooking time: 3 hours
Servings: 2

Ingredients:
- 1 lb lamb stew meat, cubed
- 1 red onion, sliced
- 1 lb spinach
- 1 can (14 oz) diced tomatoes
- 2 garlic cloves
- 2 tablespoons ginger, minced
- 2 teaspoons ground cardamom
- 6 cloves
- 2 teaspoons ground coriander
- ½ teaspoon chili powder
- 1 teaspoon garam masala
- 2 teaspoons cumin

Instructions:
1. Add all the ingredients except the spinach to a large pot, pour 1 cup water on top.

2. Bring everything to a boil, lower the heat to a simmer and cook covered for 2-3 hours.

3. Add spinach before serving, wilt it and serve.

Nutritional info (per serving):
570 calories
17.3 g fat
5 g carbohydrate
24 g protein

5.9. GOBHI PARATHAS

Gobhiparathas is a popular dish from Punjabi. It's often served in restaurants. Households in Punjabi often serve gobhiparathas for breakfast. Cooking the gobi and adding as it as a stuffing affects the taste of the parathas. You can use a hand grater to grate the gobi finely. The gratings of food processors are larger than the ones produced by hand graters. The gobi should be grated finely, or else the parathas will break. You can also serve gobhiparathas for dinner, especially if you can't be bothered to prepare an elaborate meal. Gobhiparathas can be served with mango pickle or white butter. You can also serve it with curd.

Cooking time: 25 minutes
Servings: 12

Ingredients:

- 3 cups coconut or almond flour
- 1 cup water
- 1 tablespoon ghee
- ½ cauliflower head, grated
- 1 green chili, chopped
- 1 teaspoon garam masala
- A pinch red chili powder
- Salt, to taste

Instructions:
1. Mix flour, salt and ghee in a bowl. Add water and knead until smooth dough is formed. Cover and refrigerate for 20-30 minutes.

2. Mix cauliflower and green chili in a separate bowl. Stir well to combine.

3. Now shape 2 medium sized balls from the dough. Dust with more flour. Roll both balls out to 3-4 inches circle.

4. Spread some ghee on top of each circle, top with cauliflower mixture, garam masala, red chili and salt. Press and seal the edges.

5. Dust the paratha with four and gently roll out to a size of a roti.

6. Preheat ghee in a skillet over medium heat. Add parathas and cook until browned on all sides. Serve.

Nutritional info (per serving):
84 calories
7.8 g fat
3.8 g carbohydrate
2.9 g protein

5.10. KERALA STYLE EGG CURRY

Kerala style egg curry is a delicious quick-fix meal that you can serve to your guests. It can be served with neerdosa, appam, puttu or poori. This dish is rich in protein and combines potatoes, eggs, and spices with coconut milk gravy. Your kids will definitely love the creamy gravy and soft potatoes. Egg curry is nutritious so that it can give them energy. The flavors and aroma of the dish are also tempting. Potatoes pair well with different kinds of protein, so its addition to this dish is just perfect. You can adjust the spices to suit your spice level.

Cooking time: 30 minutes
Servings: 4

Ingredients:

- 4 eggs, hard boiled, halved
- 1 onion, sliced
- 3 green chilies, chopped
- 1 tomato, chopped
- 1 ½ cups coconut milk, medium thick
- ¾ cup thick coconut milk
- 2 sprigs curry leaves
- ¼ teaspoon mustard seeds
- 1 ½ teaspoons garlic paste
- 1 ½ teaspoons ginger paste
- ¼ teaspoon turmeric powder
- 1 tablespoon kashmiri chili powder
- 1 ½ teaspoons garam masala
- ½ teaspoon fennel powder
- 1 teaspoon pepper powder
- 1 tablespoon coriander powder
- Vegetable oil
- Salt, to taste

Instructions:
1. Preheat oil in a skillet over medium heat. Add mustard seeds, onion, green chili, curry leaves and salt. Cook for about 5 minutes.

2. Add ginger and garlic paste, sauté for 1-2 minutes.

3. Add turmeric powder, chilli powder, pepper powder, coriander powder, garam masala and fennel powder. Cook for 3-4 minutes.

4. Add tomato, sauté for 2-3 minutes more. Add medium thick coconut milk and salt. Mix well to combine.

5. Add eggs and cook for 10 minutes coating the eggs. Add thick coconut milk and stir well until combined. Serve.

Nutritional info (per serving):
288 calories
29 g fat
7 g carbohydrate
13 g protein

6.SIDES

6.1.ROASTED LEMONY GARLICKY BROCCOLI

Are you looking for a unique way to cook broccoli? Roasted broccoli with lemon and garlic can be served alongside dinner. It's a flavorful side dish that complements everything from seafood to meat, casseroles, and pasta. You can top it with grated parmesan cheese for an extra burst of flavor. Broccoli is already good on its own, so it doesn't need a lot of toppings to satisfy your taste buds. If you want to add something to this side dish, you can top it with toasted nuts for that extra crunch. You can serve roasted broccoli with stews, crab cakes, and baked macaroni.

Cooking time: 20 minutes
Servings: 8

Ingredients:
- 2 heads broccoli, broken into florets
- 2 tablespoons olive oil
- 2 teaspoons salt
- 6 garlic cloves, minced
- 1/2 lemon, juiced

Instructions:
1. Preheat oven to 400 F.

2. Toss all the ingredients in a bowl. Spread out the broccoli florets ona baking tray lined with parchment paper.

3. Bake for 15-20 minutes and serve.

Nutritional info (per serving):
71 calories
12 g fat
6 g carbohydrate
8 g protein

6.2. CUCUMBER PEANUT SALAD

Cucumber peanut salad is a refreshing combination of peanuts and cucumber. You don't have to be a professional chef to make your cucumber peanut salad. This recipe won't require a lot of your time. You can make it within 10 minutes. Cucumber peanut salad is perfect for summer., and is loaded with fresh flavors. This recipe is also vegan and vegetarian-friendly as well as gluten-free. You only need to cook the dressing with mustard seeds and hot oil. If you want to add extra flavors, you can throw in some MatkiUssal. This recipe can be served as a quick lunch as well.

Cooking time: 10 minutes
Servings: 4

Ingredients:
- 2 cucumber, sliced
- ½ cup fresh cilantro, chopped
- ¼ cup roasted sesame seeds
- 2 tablespoons fresh lime juice
- 1 ½ tablespoons fish sauce
- 1 tablespoon coconut aminos
- 1 tablespoon apple cider vinegar
- 1 garlic clove, minced
- 1/4 teaspoon red pepper flakes
- 2 teaspoons sesame oil
- Salt, pepper, to taste

Instructions:
1. Mix lime juice, fish sauce, coconut aminos, vinegar, garlic, chilies or pepper flakes, sesame oil, salt and pepper in a bowl.

2. In a separate bowl, mix cucumber, cilantro and sesame seeds. Add dressing and toss to coat. Serve.

Nutritional info (per serving):

127 calories
8.3 g fat
6.3 g carbohydrate
4 g protein

6.3.GUACAMOLE

Guacamole is easy to make with salt and ripe avocados. It can be served with tortilla chips. A small amount of lemon or lime juice will help balance the fruit's richness. You can also add tomatoes, chopped cilantro or onion. Use only ripe avocados that are perfectly ripe. If you use avocados that are too ripe, the taste of your guacamole will be off. If your avocados that are not ripe enough, it will be bland and hard. Gently press the outside of the fruit to check its ripeness. If there's a little give, the fruit is ripe. If there's no give, the fruit isn't ripe yet.

Cooking time: 10 minutes
Servings: 4

Ingredients:
- 1 avocado
- 2 teaspoons lime juice
- 1/4 teaspoon ground cumin
- 1 garlic clove, crushed
- 1/8 teaspoon chilli powder
- 1/8 teaspoon smoked paprika
- 1 tablespoon cilantro, chopped
- 2 tablespoons scallions, sliced
- 1 tablespoon sour cream
- ¼ teaspoon salt
- A pinch pepper

Instructions:
1. Scoop the avocado flesh into a bowl and add lime juice.
2. Mash the avocado with a fork and add the remaining ingredients and mix well. Serve.

Nutritional info (per serving):
115 calories
10 g fat

7 g carbohydrate
12 g protein

6.4. MILLIE AUR JULIE WALI SABJI

Millie aurjuliewalisabji is one of the recipes that you can whip up in a hurry when there are no lentils or vegetables in your kitchen or when you're tired. Even a newbie can make this dish. It goes well with roti, chapatti, plain rice, and phulka. The use of herbs and spices make this dish super healthy and delicious. Millie aurjuliewalisabji is quite generic, so you can tweak it to suit your taste. You can also add boiled eggs or green peas to this dish. Curry powder or garam masala will make it more flavorful.

Cooking time: 40 minutes
Servings: 4

Ingredients:

- 2 onion, chopped
- ¼ cup coconut
- 1 cup carrots, diced
- ¼ cup cauliflower florets
- ¼ cup beans, chopped
- 2 oz paneer, cubed
- 2 tablespoons oil
- ½ teaspoon cumin seeds
- ¼ teaspoon asafetida
- 4 curry leaves
- 2 green chillies
- 3 dry red chillies
- 2 bay leaves
- ½ tablespoon ginger garlic paste
- 6 tomatoes, blended
- 1 teaspoon red chili powder
- ¼ teaspoon black pepper
- 1 teaspoon amchoor powder
- 1 teaspoon garam masala
- 1 teaspoon sambhar masala
- ¼ teaspoon sugar

- A handful coriander, chopped
- ½ teaspoon corn flour
- ¼ cup bell pepper, diced
- 2 tablespoons coconut milk
- Salt, black pepper, to taste

Instructions:
1. Preheat oil in a skillet over medium heat. Add cauliflower and carrots, fry for 3-4 minutes. Add beans and cook for 1-2 minutes more. Remove to a plate.

2. Add paneer and cook until browned on all sides.

3. Ina separate skillet, preheat oil too. Add onion and cook for 3-4 minutes. Add coconut and cook for 1-2 minutes more. Transfer to a blender and puree until smooth.

4. Add more oil to the pan. Add cumin seeds, asafetida, curry leaves, green chillies and dry red chillies. Also add bay leaves and stir well. Add garlic paste, stir again, cook for 30 seconds.

5. Add onion and coconut paste and cook for 1-2 minutes. Add tomato paste, season with salt and bring to a boil.

6. Add masalas to the mixture and stir well. Add the vegetables and beans mixture, add paneer and the remaining ingredients. Cook for 5-10 minutes over low heat. Serve.

Nutritional info (per serving):
376 calories

14 g fat
6.7 g carbohydrate
14 g protein

6.5.CHEESE AND CREAM SPINACH

This dish is the perfect appetizer for any party. Mozzarella, cream cheese, and parmesan make this recipe deliciously cheesy. You can top it with French-fried onions to add flavor to the dish. Cheese and cream spinach also make a yummy diner side dish that you can prepare in just 10 minutes. It is low carb and keto-friendly, so you can eat it without feeling any guilt. Cheese and cream spinach goes well with pork, steak, and poultry. It is perfect comfort food, which you can also serve it for holiday meals. Top it with a dash of nutmeg to highlight the taste of the spinach.

Cooking time: 10 minutes
Servings: 4

Ingredients:
- 3 tablespoons butter
- 4 garlic cloves, minced
- 10 oz baby spinach, chopped
- ½ cup heavy cream
- 3 oz cream cheese
- 1 teaspoon Italian seasoning
- ¼ teaspoon sea salt
- ¼ teaspoon black pepper

Instructions:
1. Preheat butter in a pan over medium heat. Add minced garlic and cook until fragrant.

2. Add spinach. Cook for 2-4 minutes, until wilted.

3. Add heavy cream, cream cheese, sea salt, black pepper and Italian seasoning. Cook until cream cheese melts, stirring constantly. Keep cooking until cheese thickens. Serve.

Nutritional info (per serving):
274 calories

27 g fat
5 g carbohydrate
4 g protein

7.DESSERTS

7.1.KESAR KALAKAND

Kesarkalakand boasts a rich taste that is perfect for various occasions such as festivals, birthdays, anniversaries, and family functions. You can also make this dessert for vrat or fasting. This Indian dessert is made by combining crumbled paneer, sugar, reduced full-cream milk, and milk powder. You can make it in less than 30 minutes. It's flavored with cardamom powder and saffron and topped with nuts. You can serve this dessert after it sets and top it with rose petals. Store Kesarkalakand in the fridge and consume it within 1 week.

Cooking time: 15 minutes
Servings: 24

Ingredients:
- 2 ½ cups packed Paneer, grated
- 1 can (14 oz) condensed milk
- 4 tablespoons milk powder
- ½ teaspoon cardamom powder
- 3 tablespoons nuts of choice, chopped
- A pinch saffron strands
- 1 tablespoon dried rose petals, for serving

Instructions:
1. Mix about 2 tablespoons warm milk with saffron and let ewst.

2. Prepare a baking pan and line with parchment paper.

3. Mix paneer, condensed milk, milk powder and cardamom in a pan. Place over medium heat, cook until the mixture loosens in the heat.

4. Reduce the heat to low and cook for 15 minutes, stirring frequently.

5. Pour the mixture into the prepared baking pan, smooth well with a spoon.

6. Drizzle the saffron and some of the milk on top. Top with chopped nuts and rose petals.

7. Let cool and cover, refrigerate for at least 2 hours.

8. Cut into pieces and serve.

Nutritional info (per serving):
78 calories
13 g fat
1.3 g carbohydrate
2.7 g protein

7.2. ALMOND WALNUT CHOCOLATE MOUSSE

Almond walnut chocolate mousse is healthy and filling that you can serve as a dessert, snack, or special breakfast. The cocoa powder gives the desert a rich chocolaty taste, while the almonds and walnuts create a crunchy and tasty crust. Your kids will love this almond walnut chocolate mousse. It's a healthier alternative to cakes and other junk food that kids usually eat at school without your knowledge. Walnuts are rich in nutrients and omega-6 fats. Give this dessert a shot and enjoy its delicious taste and texture! It is also a perfect dessert for cuddly situations as well as romantic dinners.

Cooking time: 5 minutes
Servings: 4

Ingredients:
- flesh of 2 ripe avocados
- ¼ cup regular cocoa powder
- ¼ cup melted chocolate chips
- 3 tablespoons almond milk
- ½ teaspoon pure vanilla extract
- ¼ cup maple syrup
- ¼ cup almonds and walnuts mix, chopped

Instructions:
1. Combine all ingredients except for nuts in a blender or food processor until completely smooth.

2. Fold in nuts and stir well to combine. Cover and refrigerate for at least 2 hours. Serve.

Nutritional info (per serving):
146 calories
13.1 g fat
11.1 g carbohydrate
3.1 g protein

7.3. COCONUT AND CREAM BARFI

Coconut and cream barfi is a delectable and soft fudge made with sugar syrup mixture and freshly grated coconut. Condensed milk has been added to the recipe in recent years. The combination of sugar syrup mixture and condensed milk gives the dessert a chewy texture. If you want to create a soft barfi, you can use cream instead of condensed milk. Doing so also reduces cooking time. You can finish this recipe in less than fifteen minutes. This means that you can spend more time doing other things. There's no reason why you shouldn't try this recipe. Grab your spatula and get started!

Cooking time: 15 minutes
Servings: 12

Ingredients:
- 3 cups coconut, grated
- 1 ½ cups sugar
- 3/4 cup heavy whipping cream
- 3 tablespoons confectioner's sugar
- 1/2 teaspoon freshly ground cardamom
- Ghee, for greasing
- Pistachios, chopped, for serving

Instructions:
1. Preheat a non-stick kadhai over medium heat and add grated coconut, sugar and cream. Mix well till well combined.

2. Cook until the mixture is golden, stirring all the time.

3. Remove from heat and add cardamom powder and confectioners' sugar, stir well.

4. Grease a pan with ghee, pour the mixture into the pan. Sprinkle with nuts and let rest for at least 1 hour in the fridge, Cut into pieces and serve.

Nutritional info (per serving):
232 calories
19 g fat
6 g carbohydrate
12 g protein

7.4. KETO ROCKY ROAD

Keto rocky road is a low carb treat packed with pecans and marshmallows covered in rich chocolate coating. It is creamy smooth and completely sugar-free! You can make this treat around Easter time or have it anytime you are craving for a healthy and luscious dessert. Keto rocky road is also loaded with shredded coconut and hazelnuts. Some prep work is required if you want to make this recipe. You have to make and freeze the marshmallows one day ahead to let them dry out properly. The marshmallows need to be chopped and frozen to prevent them from becoming goo. Everything will be worth it once you a bite of your homemade keto rocky road.

Cooking time: 5 minutes
Servings: 2

Ingredients:
- 1 cup grass-fed butter
- 2 cups marshmallows
- 2 cups hazelnuts
- ¼ cup almonds
- ¼ cup freeze dried blueberries
- 14 oz dark chocolate chips

Instructions:
1. Add hazelnuts and almonds to a dry skillet and toast for about 5 minutes over medium heat.

2. Line a baking sheet with parchment paper. Melt chocolate chips and butter in a bowl, stir well until smooth. Let cool to room temperature.

3. Add nuts, marshmallows and blueberries to the batter and pour into the baking sheet. Cover and refrigerate for at least 2-3 hours.

4. Cut into pieces and serve.

Nutritional info (per serving):
155 calories
16 g fat
7 g carbohydrate
5 g protein

7.5. CHOCOLATE AND COFFEE ICE CREAM

This dessert is a dream come true for coffee and chocolate lovers. It offers the perfect combination of chocolate and coffee. If you want to get the best coffee flavor, you can use whole coffee beans. However, there are also instant coffees with great flavor. Don't be bothered by the dark color because the heavy cream will lighten up the color a bit and maintain the coffee flavor. If you love dark chocolate, here's your chance to mix it with coffee. You can have your ice cream as soft serve or transfer it to a container and store it in the fridge to make it harder.

Cooking time: 15 minutes
Servings: 2

Ingredients:

- 1 ¾ cups heavy whipping cream
- 1/2 unsweetened almond milk
- 1 ½ teaspoons instant coffee
- 3 egg yolks
- 2 oz sugar free dark chocolate, chopped
- ½ teaspoon vanilla extract
- ¼ teaspoon xanthan gum
- 2 tablespoons sweetener of choice

Instructions:
1. Mix cream, almond milk, sweetener and coffee in a saucepan over medium heat. Stir until sweetener and coffee dissolve.

2. Whisk the egg yolks in a bowl. Slowly add the hot cream mixture, whisking continuously. Pour the mixture to the pan and cook for 3-4 minutes, stirring constantly.

3. Let cool for about 20 minutes. Wrap tightly in plastic wrap and chill for at least 3 hours.

4. Add vanilla extract. Sprinkle with the xanthan gum and whisk vigorously to combine. Pour the mixture into an ice cream maker and process as per the manufacturer's directions.

5. Add the chopped chocolate. Transfer the mixture to an airtight container and freeze until firm.

Nutritional info (per serving):
234 calories
22.7 g fat
4.7 g carbohydrate
5 g protein

7.6. KETO MACAROON

Coconut macaroons are crisp on the outside and soft on the inside. These plain yet tasty treats have a long shelf life. Coconut macaroons are the perfect treat to give away during the holiday season as you can bake them ahead of time. It's easy to make. You only need to mix the ingredients and bake them in an oven. Once it's done, you can share your homemade coconut macaroons with your family and friends. This treat is a sure hit with both kids and adults. If you want to make a simple dessert that will put a smile on your family's faces, you should try making coconut macaroons.

Cook time: 8 minutes
Servings: 10

Ingredients:
- ¼ cup almond flour
- ½ cup shredded coconut
- 2 tablespoons Swerve
- 1 tablespoon vanilla extract
- 1 tablespoon coconut oil
- 3 egg whites

Instructions:
1. Preheat the oven to 400F.

2. Mix almond flour, coconut and swerve in a bowl.

3. Add coconut oil to a sauce pan and melt over low heat. Add vanilla, stir to combine.

4. Whisk egg whites until stiff peaks form. Slowly add egg whites to the flour mixture, mix well to incorporate.

5. Pour the mixture into the muffin cups and bake for 8 minutes. Let cool before serving.

Nutritional info (per serving):
134 calories
13.8 g fat
3.7 g carbohydrate
1.3 g protein

7.7. SHRIKHAND

Shrikhand is made with powdered sugar and hung curd. It's a sweet dish that is regularly served with puri. Shrikhand has flavoring and dry fruits added to it. It is popular in Maharashtra and Gujarat as a side dessert and as a dessert. You only need 3 ingredients to make Shrikhand – powdered sugar, fresh plain yoghurt, and your desired flavoring. The ingredients are very easy to find, so you can easily prepare this dessert. If you don't want any extra flavoring, you can keep your Shrikhand plain. Make sure everything is mixed thoroughly. You can add other ingredients to create a different flavor.

Cook time: 10 minutes + chilling time
Servings: 2

Ingredients:
- 3/4 cup Greek yogurt
- 2 tablespoons Erythritol
- few strands saffron crushed into mortar and pestle
- 1 teaspoon milk
- 1/4 teaspoon green cardamom seeds powder
- 4-5 cashew nuts chopped finely
- 4-5 almonds chopped finely
- 4-5 pistachios chopped finely, optional

Instructions:
1. Dissolve crushed saffron in the warm milk.

2. Put Greek yogurt, Erythritol into a bowl and stir till everything is combined well.

3. Add saffron milk, cardamom powder, chopped nuts and mix well.

4. Put it into a refrigerator for couple of hours before serving.

Nutritional info (per serving):
287 calories
4.5 g fat
4.8 g carbohydrate
14.6 g protein

7.8. BADAM KULFI

GulabiKulfi is an ice cream that originated in India. You can prepare this dessert for dinner or your snack. If you're going to use full-fat milk, you should reduce it on an even flame and add condensed milk or khoya to make it rich. Cardamons and nuts are then added. Kulfi can be flavored with different fruits, spices, and nuts. The ice cream is rich and thick, and its flavor is denser than English ice creams. If you want an Indian inspired flavor, you should try making your own GulabiKulfi. Your kids will love the unique texture and taste of this ice cream.

Cook time: 4 hours 20 minutes
Servings: 4

Ingredients:

- 2 cups ground almonds, blanched & peeled
- 2 cups condensed milk
- 1/2 cup milk
- 8 tablespoons fresh cream
- 15 strand saffron
- 6 pieces pistachios
- 2 tablespoons blanched almonds

Instructions:
1. Combine ground almonds, cream condensed milk in a large bowl and whisk until thick. Set aside.

2. Heat milk in a saucepan on a high flame and then boil it.

3. When milk starts boiling, add saffron strands and mix well. Then remove pan from the flame and let the mixture cool.

4. Once it cools, combine it with the almond mixture and stir well (the consistency should be creamy and thick).

5. Heat another pan on a moderate flame, add coarsely chopped pistachios, almonds and dry roast for a few seconds.

6. Once done, combine it with the kulfi mixture (reserve some for garnish), mix well and pour the mixture into the kulfimoulds.

7. Cover the top with a lid and keep in a freezer for 4 hours or until set.

8. Once done, remove kulfi from the mould and sprinkle with some of the reserved pistachios and almonds.

Nutritional info (per serving):
178 calories
11 g fat
7.3 g carbohydrate
12 g protein

7.9.LAUKI KI KHEER

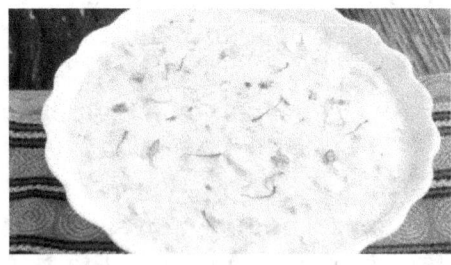

Laukikikheer is made using milk and bottle gourd. This creamy dessert doesn't require any special preparations since you only need some cream, sugar, ghee, saffron, dry fruits, milk, and fresh bottle gourd. It can be made during fasting days such as Ekadashi and Navratri. You can serve Laukikikheer on weekdays or weekends as a special dessert. If you're not using dairy milk, you can use almond milk instead. Thick coconut milk will also do. Don't boil or heat the milk too much to prevent it from curdling. Follow this recipe and enjoy this dessert with your family.

Cook time: 40 minutes
Servings: 6

Ingredients:
- 2 tablespoons ghee
- 12 almonds, crushed
- 12 cashews, crushed
- 2 cups Lauki/Bottle gourd, grated
- 4 cups full fat coconut milk
- 12 strands Saffron
- 2 tablespoons sweetener of choice
- 1 teaspoon Cardamom powder

Instructions:
1. Preheat ghee in a pan over medium heat. Add almonds and cashews and fry until browned.

2. Add grated Lauki and fry for 5-6 minutes on low heat.

3. Add milk and bring everything to a boil. Reduce the heat to low and cook until the mixture thickens.

4. Add saffron and cook on low heat for 20-25 minutes, stirring from time to time.

5. Add cardamom powder and sweetener, cook for 3-4 minutes.

6. Serve topped with almond and pistachio slivers and rose petals. Serve chilled.

Nutritional info (per serving):
115 calories
7 g fat
6 g carbohydrate
11 g protein

7.10. MUG MAIN MASTI

Mug main Masti is the perfect solution if you are looking for something that can satisfy your cravings and easy to make at the same time. After spending a lot of time in the kitchen cooking a delicious lunch for your family, you want to relax and avoid this part of the house for some time. Well, you can enjoy a sweet dessert without spending a long time in the kitchen. Mug main Masti only requires a few ingredients. Most of these ingredients are already available in your kitchen. The best thing about this dessert is that it only takes a few minutes to prepare!

Cook time: 40 minutes
Servings: 6

Ingredients:
- 2 tablespoons unsalted grass-fed butter
- 1 1/2 tablespoons cocoa powder
- 2 tablespoons erythritol
- 1 egg
- 2 tablespoons almond flour
- 1 tablespoon golden flaxseed meal
- 2 teaspoons coconut flour
- 1/2 teaspoon baking powder
- A pinch of salt

Instructions:
1. Melt butter in a bowl. Add cocoa and sweetener, mix until well combined.

2. Add egg and mix until smooth. Add the remaining ingredients and pour the batter into a mug.

3. Place a paper towel into the microwave and place the mug on top. Cook on high for 70-90 seconds. Let cool for a couple minutes and enjoy!

Nutritional info (per serving)

219 calories
17 g fat
7.5 g carbohydrate
6 g protein

Part 2

Introduction

India, South Asia's great area of land, is host to one of the largest and most powerful civilizations in the world. We are all quite mindful of the fact that the Indians are quite foodie. We always wish to speak about cooking, to eat and to try various recipes. Certainly, each and every single household in India has its own formula which they elevate from generation to generation. Yet, how much are we really conscious of Indian food history? Thus, the Indian Food Heritage journey will be discussed in this topic.

India has received a multitude of immigrants with a number of religious traditions through more than 4,000 years of recorded history. To understand the dynamics of India's native food culture, one has to know that this nation is far from culturally homogeneous. Regions and sects make up a great deal of the food. "Indian food" was invented a term that a native will probably chuckle at because such a word would be like saying "North American wine" to a wine expert. There are many places in India that have their own special cooking methods, seasonings, and fresh ingredients. Tipping its population-scale to over a billion, its food diversity is as diverse as its inhabitants.

Muslims and Hindu are the two dominant sects that most affected Indian food culture and food choices. They took out their own food practices with each movement of natives. There is the widespread practice of the vegetarian Hindu culture. In comparison, Muslim culture is the most common in meat cooking. Mughlai cuisine, kababs, nargisikaftas, biryani and favorite dishes served in the tandoor are great benefits provided by Muslim natives in India. The food in South India is mostly rice related, with a thin porridge accent named Rasam. In all South Indian cuisine, coconut is an essential component. Dosa and idli are very common foods among vegetarian from Hindu culture. Also, the Portuguese, Persians, and British contributed a great deal too Indian food. The British brought tea to India, and it is nowadays the favorite drink of many Indians.

The four main geographic types of Indian cooking are the North, East, South, and West. North India was impacted by the Mughal dynasty which held power for 300 years until they were substituted by the British in the 18th century. Naan bread, produced in a tandoor, is not native. It is the Afghani people's daily meal. Naan is not Indians' baked daily bread, but it has been a common misconception of Indian food outside the region for decades.

Among Southern Indians, specified steamed rice cakes are favorite. Rice is consumed in all meals, and lunch mostly consists of all meal courses, each filled with rice again. The Hindus are categorized into vegetarians and non-vegetarians. Their common thread in Kerala's Southern Region is coconut, which is the state's culinary mascot. The Gujarat, Maharashtra and Goa western states all have unique experiences of health. Gujarat has predominantly Muslims, Hindus, Parsis and Jains who have their own cooking methods. Parsis have a rich diet of poultry and seafood. Gujaratis are primarily veggie eaters, and Gujarat is known as one of the best places for consuming vegetarian food. Maharashtra is a large state with its Mumbai city of fame. East states are very distinct. Bengali cuisine, with fish and rice at the core of the diet, can be characterized as delicate and subtle. The order of a Bengali meal starts with a mixed vegetable dish with a bitter taste and finishes with a rich sweet dessert based on milk for which Bengali is popular. Orissa is popular for squash blossoms rolled in rice and deep-fried paste or turned into patties. Cod and other fish are in the diet too. It is very rare that chicken will be eaten here, and poultry plays a small culinary role in general. Bihar and Jharkhand love their vegetables and beans, but with their diet, they do have Western overtones like beef, pork, goat and poultry. Indian cuisine tends to be unified only by its locality from East to West, but its taste is evidently boundless.

Brief History of Traditional Indian Dishes

The past of Indian food is the background of innovation from various societies in periods of need and succession. Such dishes were created for general populous sake, while others have been imported from all over the geographies. Many of those fascinating Indian food tales are now unaware of. Some of the Traditional Indian is explained as below:

- **Petha is older than TajMahal**

Petha in Agra is the best choice to consume. The innovation is relevant to the development of the TajMahal in the Mughals. When the monumental shrine was under a building, the daily meal containing just dal and roti bored some 20,000 employees. Then Mughal Emperor Shah Jahan expressed his worry with the master architect Ustad Isa Effendi who demanded a response to the Emperor's problems from PirNaqshbandi Sahib. It is claimed that one day, during prayers, the Pir formed a trance and gave Petha's formula to Mughal. About 500 cooks then rendered Petha for the staff.

- **Dal Bati Was a Tool of Survival in Wars**

This is Rajasthan's best food to eat. The recipe of Dal Bati is a tale worth sharing with. This Rajasthani food has its roots in the popular MewarChittorgarh Fort. Bati is wheat dough fried in oil, a food that the Mewar Rajput kings needed to live in unfavorable wartime circumstances. Bati could be produced in the desert lands of Rajasthan with the few supplies and a little water available.

- **Mysore Went from Monarchy to Common**

It is South India's, iconic sweetmeat. The past of Mysore is related to the Mysore Palace kitchen of the early 20th century. In the Mysore Palace, the royal cook used to impress the King with numerous dishes. He rendered a new sweet dish one day with the mixture of chickpea flour, oil and sugar. The cook coined the word 'Mysore Paka' in a split second on being questioned the word of the sauce. 'Paka' is a Kannada word which signifies a sweet mixture.

- **Khaja is Generational of the Mauryan and Gupta Realms**

While the cooking art of creating Khaja is a moment of honor for the Orissa citizens, it is claimed that the technique was borrowed from Bihar's central highlands around 2200 years ago. Khaja's roots go back to antique Indian Gupta empires. Rajgir'sKhaja in Bihar is famed for its swelling, while Kakinada's Khaja in Andhra Pradesh is popular for its dry outside but savory within.

- **Jalebi's Culture is Not Necessarily Indian**

One of India's most famous sweet dishes, Jalebi owes its roots to West Asia. Jalebi was introduced to India in mediaeval times by the Persian-speaking invaders. This sweetmeat was called 'Kundalika' in India in the 14th century, and 'Jalavallika'. During Ramadan in Iran, the poor were given platefuls of Jalebi.

- **Dum Biryani Provided Meals in Awadh for the Needy**

According to numerous historical records, the root of biryani is the provincial capital of Hyderabad in the Nawab period. Some discussions show that biryani was initiated in the early mediaeval era during Timur's invasion of India. While biryani's origin is being discussed, Dum Biryani or Awadh's Biryani emerged in Lucknow. The Nawab of Awadh directed all the poor folks of his area to cook a meal in big handis (round-shaped brass pots) when food was scarce. A large volume of food was cooked in covered and sealed pans, with limited energy. This cooking craft has been popular as 'dum'.

Indian Food and Its Popularity in the US

Indian food is becoming increasingly common in the US. It is like a highly specialized food right now. Apart from Chinese cuisine, which is almost part of the American environment, the food network shows even more references of Indian cuisine and Indian ingredients are showing up everywhere in the US. Thanks to their wonderful taste, Indian dishes have earned popularity around the world. Several tasty Indian meals are cooked in different dining spots around the country. Various fans on a global scale have noticed the vast range of salads, appetizers, sweets, side dishes and desserts, as Indian restaurants have been expanded at an unprecedented pace, with immense popularity in every imaginable community and in every imaginable corner of the Globe.

India is the world's largest grocer of fruit. India has tremendous science and engineering potential that is rapidly being used to produce modern, popular food goods in the US. New products are still in demand, so there is tremendous potential for new products, especially in the US, where people love to eat Indian food. The success of American Indian food has also enabled a movement for Indian businesses to sell more food products to the US.

Indian cuisine is known in the world for its spices and aromatic taste. The numerous Indian restaurants in Washington DC prepare mouth-watering dishes and serve it to both the visitors and the local people in the region. Every place has unique culinary art, which is completely different from each other. These techniques were introduced to western countries and acquired enormous prominence among citizens. For special occasions, the special dish is cooked. Many international buyers have been fascinated by the spices and the different products used to cook such dishes.

It is very important to remember that there is a therapeutic benefit in most Indian spices. The most widely used herbs are turmeric, ginger and cardamom since they have therapeutic properties. This is one of the key explanations, why citizens in the US are sincerely willing to consume Indian food, claiming that the Indian food would not affect their body in any way as the spices used, have medicinal properties. In this book, you will learn the Indian Cuisine, spices often used in them, and 100 recipes, in detail.

Chapter 1: Learning the Basics of Indian Cuisine

Indian cuisine is comprised of a number of modern and conventional Indian subcontinent cuisines. Owing to the variety of land, climate, history, ethnic groups, and professions, these foods differ considerably and use herbs, vegetables, and fruits available locally. Also, Indian food is highly related to religion, particularly Hinduism, social decisions and rituals.

1.1 Indian Regional Foods - at a Glance

While presenting dishes as part of a standardized, nationalized cuisine is popular for Indian restaurants. India's food is actually as regionally unique and diverse as its people. These foods are hugely affected by the past of India, it is trading relations, and it is cultural and religious traditions. A little context on the commonalities and variations between the regional cuisines of India will transform your next Indian meal into an entertaining, and profoundly gratifying.

While Indian food is highly local unique, there are some popular ties that connect the numerous cuisine practices. Indian cuisine across the nation is highly reliant on sauces, which are sauce-like sauce or soup-like meat, potato, or cheese dishes. However, the unique spice mixtures, liquidity amount, and ingredients are decided by regional choice. In general, Indian cuisine is also highly dependent upon agriculture, while Southern Indian areas use rice more strongly than other places. Both regional foods depend on legumes or "pulses." Indian cuisine can use a wider range of peas than any other menu selections: Red lentils, black gram, peas or yellow gramme, black gramme, and green gramme are used in a variety of Indian dishes as a whole, broken, or ground in flour. Add tartness to meals that do not use eggs, legumes, and nutrition to vegan diets.

The rich usage of spices is probably the most distinguishing feature of Indian food. Indian spice blends mostly use up to five separate spices, occasionally adding ten or more. Garam masala is a common mixture of spices, cardamom, cinnamon, and clove, with the specific spices differing by area and personal recipe.

- **Observations Indicated: Commerce and Invasion**

In India's cuisine, the cultural effect of trade is clear, with unique areas and dishes carrying the sign of international influence. Arab and Canadian traders strongly desired India's spices; in return, India obtained several commodities that profoundly shaped its food heritage. Portuguese merchants carried in New World products such as onions, peppers, and chilies, which were profoundly incorporated into Indian dishes. Coffee was carried by Arab merchants.

India's occupation times have also significantly influenced the nature of its delicacies. Mughal conquerors, who ruled India between both the early 1500s and late 1600s, introduced Persian spices and traditions in India's culinary culture. The influence is noticeable in the use of cheese and milk in sauces, the use of meat and nuts in salads, and in particular in salads.

Although the arrival of the British in India exposed the nation to soup and tea; it had no effect on its food. However, the imperial incorporation of local food into British society has profoundly influenced Indian food translation abroad. Tikka Masala, a flavorful sauce on many Indian menus, is originally an Anglo-Indian invention and is widely called as "Britain's true national dish". Even European conceptions of Indian "curry"-the term applies to a myriad of garlicky and stew-like meals-are inferred from British understanding of Indian cuisine.

- **India: Large Community**

The population of India is incredibly complex, with cultural traditions deeply shaped by ethnic and religious specificities. Ayurvedic traditions also exercised control on Indian cuisine in particular by trying to dictate spice combinations and cooking methods, stressing the balance between brain, body, and spirit. This theory is a popular influence in Indian cuisine, as per religion and cultural characteristics. Around one-third of the population in India is vegetarian, determined by its

Hindu, Jain or Buddhist values. Consequently, a large portion of the countrywide Indian dishes is without beef. In addition, religious traditions influence other dietary prohibitions that form India's cuisine: Hindu believers abstain from meat, since cattle are holy in this religion, whereas Muslims claim that pork is impure and they never eat it. Depending on a region's prevailing religious beliefs, cooking in a given area can exclude those ingredients to conform to religious rules.

- **Northern Indian Kitchen**

Northern Indian cuisine, possibly the most widespread cuisine form found from outside India, demonstrates a clear Mughal influence. It is distinguished by strong dairy consumption: milk, paneer (a mild Indian cheese), butter, and yoghurt are all commonly used in Northern dishes. A famous Northern treat is samosas and sometimes beef. Clay ovens identified as tandoors are common in the North, offering their distinct barbecue flavor to dishes such as naan. A considerable number of Northern foods appear daily on Indian menus. Dal or PaneerMakhani is common vegetarian dishes, comprising of dal or paneer fried in a creamy tomato sauce, oignons, mango dust, and curry powder. Korma, another Northern Indian staple meal, is a smooth curry with coconut milk or yoghurt, cumin, cilantro and tiny quantities of cashews or walnuts. It can be eaten with numerous meats, typically poultry or lamb, but often beef and a vegan dish with paneer.

- **West Indian Kitchen**

Western local food is characterized by its region's political and cultural particularities. The coastal area of Maharashtra is known for their milk-dominant seafood and coconut cuisine. Gujarati food is mainly vegetarian, and due to strong influences, has an inherent sweetness to most of its dishes. Since this region's dry climate reported to be low veggies, this region is well renowned for its chutneys, common Indian condiments which use fried, fresh, or marinated fruits and vegetables with sweet, sour, or spicy flavors. Goa served as a large port and colony of commerce for Portugal, culminating in a rare mix of Indian and Portuguese cuisine features. Goa cuisine utilizes more commonly than other different foods in India, utilizing beef and pork. Vinegar is also a distinctive component in Goa cuisine. Its coastal presence results in the proliferation of coconut milk, coconut powder and fish in Goa cuisine.

- **East Indian Kitchen**

Eastern local food is renowned mainly for their sweets. Not only are these desserts preferred by other states of India, but they are also found in restaurants. Their delicate sweet is rendering an outstanding finale to dinner. Rasgulla is a common sweet treat, consisting of balls of semolina and cheese curd, boiled in light sugar syrup. Eastern dishes prefer mustard seeds and mustard oil, bringing a pleasant smell to the dishes. In Eastern cuisine rice and seafood are also prominent. Eastern foods, on the whole, are spiced more strongly than from certain countries.

- **Indian Southern Food**

Southern Indian food is not usually seen on many menus of restaurants and is somewhat distinct from other areas. Their "curries" vary greatly in their appearance and may usually be classified as per the drier quality, or those preferring a more stew-like or soupy appearance.

Poriyals, dried curries made up of a mixture of veggies and seasoning, complement the rice food. Sambars are basically pea and vegetable stews with a tamarind taste, which are soupier than curries from many other countries, but smoother than rasams. Rasams in their quality is somewhat comparable to soups, and comprise mostly of tomatoes, tamarind, and a variety of spices. Kootus is more comparable to curries seen in other regions, but instead of being fluffy like the North's dairy-based curries, kootus gets its strength from drained lentils.

Southern Indian food is renowned for its exquisite fried or griddle-cooked sweets, in addition to curry-style dishes. Dosas consist of a broad crepe. They are normally packed with curries of veggies, curries, or seasonings. Idli is fried delicacy identical to savory doughnuts, which are eaten as sambar and rasam side dishes. Apart from restaurants directly serving Southern Indian cuisine, pappadams, fried crispy rice cookies commonly spiced with black peppercorns, are the only South Indian food that are often seen in Indian restaurants.

1.2 Features of Indian Food

Indian food has penetrated all territorial frontiers and entered the international territory. Everyone seems to recognize and love the Tandoori chicken or the Pavbhaji or the Kesarkulfi today. Foodies worldwide are massive fans of both vegetarian and non-vegetarian Indian delicacies.

- **The Pattern Present**

More and more customers are visiting the world's prestigious Indian restaurants and eating famous Indian culinary delights. In the food chain, Indian food is growing rapidly by the day. Tandoori is strongly in request all over the world. North Indian food is extremely delicious. The wonderful Tandoori snacks like the Tandoori Chicken ChickenReshmi Kebabs and much more you will never get over.

- **Astonishing Richness**

Owing to its exceptional variety Indian food is becoming famous over the years. Indian food has plenty for any form of taste bud to satisfy. Some citizens are interested in South Indian delicacies; some are intrigued by Punjabi delights, some are obsessed with Rajasthani or Goa food, Parsi food or mouth-watering Bengali foods. A new life has been granted to Indian street food by adding a few fusion variants.

- **Food the Unstoppable Ratio**

Most Indian foods are cooked in such a way that the nutritious content of all the products is preserved and is not compromised due to the cooking method. Indian cuisine gets its true experience and tastes owing to a number of spices. These spices are good for the skin. It offers pickles and greens in various parts of India. Their flavors are special to the area, but they can activate your taste buds.

1.3 Essentials of Indian Foods in your Diet and Its Benefits

Taking into account considerations, we have arranged an important Indian food that must be part of every diet. Remember that if you are struggling from any health condition, please ask your doctor what you can take from this chart and cannot.

- **Fruits**

Many typical fruits of Indian heritage are perfect for you. They include all sorts of essential vitamins and minerals which are important to us. You can consume daily seasonal and annual fruits, such as strawberries, bananas, pomegranates, pineapples, etc. People with such health problems ought to avoid certain fruits but, for the normal citizen, these are the ideal healthy food that can supplement the fried chip bag. Health advantages Fruits provides:

- Fruits are suppliers of various under-consumed vital nutrients, including calcium, dietary fiber and vitamin C.
- Typically most fruits are poor in sugar, salt and energy.
- As you consume fruit, the energy production rises in no time; it is one of the fruit's main advantages that we can include in our hectic schedules.
- Not only does the fiber content in the fruit have a genius relaxing effect, but it also helps you feel complete when incorporating bulk protein to your diet.

- **Chilies**

New chilies, even more than other vegetables, are an outstanding rich in vitamin C. If you want spicy cuisine, you are here for luck. There are plenty of less "hard" chilies accessible for those averse to intense spicy recipes that can have the same advantages without the burning feeling. Even chilies are improving metabolism. Chilies wellness advantages:

- Chili provides up to 7 times the amount of orange vitamin C, which has a variety of health benefits like combating sinus inflammation, improving metabolism, which relieving migraines and heart, joint and nerve discomfort.
- Chili has traditionally been used to minimize bio-contamination of food and is often considered a possible weight reduction metabolic accelerator.
- It can also play a part in managing leukemia and removing lung cancer.

- **Beans**

They provide a fantastic source of protein, calcium, magnesium, and folic acid. They are flexible too, helping you to prepare loads of Indian dishes. They also go along for other community's cuisines-from Asian to the USA. Beans Benefits:

- Beans are "heart safe" since they produce reduce cholesterol levels of soluble fiber.
- The bulk of beans are around 2 to 3% fat and do not produce cholesterol unless cooked or packed with other products.
- Beans packed with fiber, avoiding acid reflux will foster regularity.
- The daily intake of beans will reduce the likelihood of cardiovascular disease.

- **Garlic**

Not only is garlic savory, but it is also often known for its numerous medicinal powers. It is a key natural source of antimicrobial agents. For garlic's nutritional benefits:

- Garlic produces a Labeled Allicin compound with strong healing uses.
- Frequent application of garlic (in diet or raw) tends to reduce total cholesterol because of Allicin's antioxidant property.
- The exhilarating properties of garlic safeguard the body from free radicals and slow down collagen depletion leading to loss of conductivity in ageing skin.

- **Spices**

Since ancient times Indian spices have become world-renowned. In addition to their amazing flavor and tastes, several spices are good for you too. Haldi or turmeric has soothing powers, helps to lower cholesterol, and avoids blood clots which may contribute to heart attacks. Cardamom improves metabolism while garam masala ingredients comprise various levels of nutrients, thus facilitating digestion as well. Spices Nutritional advantages:

- Many herbs and spices often provide more antioxidants to suppress the disease than vegetables and fruits.
- Cinnamon has a potent anti-diabetic activity and reduces blood sugar levels.
- Turmeric consists of curcumin, a material with significant antioxidant effects
- Ginger has anti-inflammatory action and may relieve nausea.

- **Paneer**

It is a big part of the vegetarian diet, but it is frequently eaten also by non-vegetarians. Paneer is a flexible meal that lends itself well to several various types of dishes. You can also stop the muscle mass-heavy variety produced from whole milk. Home-made breadcrumbs made of milk produce fewer fatty acids and cholesterol and are much better for you. But can also maintain the large amino and calcium concentrations. Paneer Advantages:

- Up to now, maybe popular knowledge, but paneer is a rich source of protein, particularly for vegetarian diets that do not get their meat intake.
- Sincepaneer is composed of protein, it steadily absorbs energy into the bloodstream, ensuring that it does not induce a spike in one's blood sugar levels, nor does it provide an immediate rise that will soon decrease.
- Besides being high in protein, paneer is a fantastic source of linoleic — a fatty acid that helps to shed weight by growing the mechanism of burning fat in the body.
- Avoids numerous disorders of the body, such as osteoporosis, knee discomfort and dental issues such as rotting of the teeth and gums.

- **Flour and Rice**

White rice is the most widely-eaten grain in India. You can, though, aim to turn to brown rice, since it incorporates more protein, making it a safer option. The switch to whole wheat flour has become more popular. Even for other wheat items like bread, you should suggest doing the same. Health advantages, which Rice and Flour provide:

- Our bodies require insoluble fibers to help them get rid of waste, so if constipation is an issue, rice and flour — particularly brown rice flour — will help alongside nuts, beans and vegetables such as cabbage— all foods that provide most of the fiber.
- Rice and flour are high in protein, with an advanced rank of B vitamins.
- Dietary fiber is an integral portion of every diet. Rice contains dietary fiber and helps to transfer waste products via the digestive tract.

- **Pulses**

The Indian diet is incredibly high in grains. The main instances are rice and pasta but note that pulses are an important part of our staple. Luckily, there are so many varieties of pulses accessible that diversity can always be preserved in your diet. Pulses are abundant in nutritious fibers and nutrients A, B, C and E. Even they produce minerals such as calcium and iron. Over everything, they are the primary source of nutrition in a vegetarian diet. Pulses health advantages:

- The use of more pulses in your eating habits can reduce your risk of heart disease.
- Pulses are the item with a lot of sugar. The sugar content lists the diet in terms of how it influences blood sugar.
- Pulses often render the protein a safe and cheap source.

- **Leafy Vegetables**

In the Indian diet, green leafy vegetables already are common. Yet they can be placed to further use. During the whole year Spinach is found throughout the region. Cabbages are also available in several areas throughout the year, too. Furthermore, hundreds of different types of leafy greens are just ready to include in your diet, depending on where in the world you reside. Leafy Vegetation has health advantages:

- Mustard and Kale greens aid reduce cholesterol.
- Leafy greens maintain good vision and reduce the likelihood of cataracts and improve the clarity you can see.
- They help to feed the body and create electricity.
- They have a mildly acidic taste: It represents their elevated calcium levels.

- **Eggs Proceed**

Although they are not necessarily a choice for vegetarian diets, they are excellent protein sources. The yolk does produce cholesterol – even if you are careful about eating the whole thing, the egg-white will help the body get the necessary minerals and nutrients. You can add eggs to almost every plate. Health advantages that Eggs provide:

- Eggs provide a very great method of free, high-quality protein.
- Feeding small kid's just one egg per day for six months, coupled with a decreased sugar-sweetened diet, can help them reach a healthy height.
- Eggs are rich in cholesterol but do not negatively impact cholesterol throughout the tissue.

- Eggs are high in some nutrients which support cardiac protection.

1.4 Health Benefits of Consuming Indian Food

The use of spices like onion, turmeric, ginger and garlic in the recipe contributes to several health advantages such as better cholesterol, lower risk of cancer and better kidney function. While we know that Indian food has several medical advantages, including spices and vegetables, you may be shocked that Indian food is not always safe. Most Indian cuisine is plant-based. Research shows there are several positive effects of consuming a plant-based diet. Some of these advantages are listed below:

- **A healthy Vegetarian Diet**

Indian dishes are perfect nutritious recipes, using a wide range of vegetables, legumes, and grains. The mixture of rice that helps you to get full protein. Since Indian ingredients use a variety of foods every day, all the minerals and vitamins found in different plants are more likely to be collected.

There are several nutrients and antioxidants in the vegetables in these dishes that are good for health, liver and brain. The Sulphur compounds present in garlic, cauliflower, and cabbage, for example, help detoxify the body from mycotoxins and toxic toxins.

- **Anti-Inflammatory Effect**

Turmeric and other spices give anti-inflammatory properties and reduce the likelihood of several chronic disorders. They frequently help relieve inflammation.
Other spices minimize inflammation, improve metabolism, aid weight control and aid detoxify the body. Often, cinnamon tends to control blood sugar levels. If you want your Indian dish to be hot and spicy, the chili is your buddy not just for your taste sense but also for your general health. Chilies are accessed of vitamin C and vitamin A.

- **Higher Concentrations of Fiber**

Good sources of both soluble and insoluble fibers are chickpeas, green vegetables, corn, grains, lentils, green beans etc. When immersed in water, soluble fibers from the peas and beans form a gel-like material. It plays a significant role in reducing your cholesterol levels and regulating your blood sugar levels. Insoluble dietary fiber facilitates regularity in the intestines and avoids indigestion.

- **Ghee Wellness Facilities**

In reality, ghee is nutritious, and if used correctly in balance, it has healing characteristics. Pure cow ghee is a key product in Indian and Ayurvedic medicinal cooking. You will use ghee as an alternative technique to butter, palm oil and hydrolyzed fat on the market. The explanation is because ghee's chemical composition is more robust than olive oil, and it does not quickly flame or get rancid. The concern for much on the market vegetable oil is that the molecular structure starts to break down during the process of heating. They quickly get oxidized and create several complications in the body by growing the number of free radicals. And you actually even know yourself how awful saturated fat is. Clarified butter or ghee, on the other side, helps guard against the toxins and supplies important fatty acids for the hormone development in the body. Ghee decreases inflammation, facilitates nutrition and improves metabolism as per Ayurveda.

1.5 How is Home Cooked Indian Food Different from Restaurant Food?

South Asian cuisine is salty, fatty, wholesome and absolutely delicious cuisine. Indian cuisine is a significant feature of U.S.-Asian life, whether in the warmth of their own homes or at a local restaurant. Eating out, however, was not a practice among the prior eras of South Asians who were settling in the US. Many saw it as something they did not do back home, an unnecessary privilege, distrusting the recipes or culinary style of 'outside' cuisine, believing the cuisine was designed for the English palate and classifying it as an elite practice. It was the custom to prepare at home, only rarely did US-Asian family go out to dinner. Many stayed as extended families in the same home for up to three families and dining out was not even a choice.
Today, in Indian restaurants, young people of USA-Asians are dining out more, bringing families out for dinner, getting take-outs and not preparing as much at home as in the past. The notion of dining out in Asian Americans is, therefore, a question of preference and culture, not hindered by disparities between generations.

And What Might be better? Home Eating or Out?

Many USA Asians also love home-made food as they feel that it is unique because of the raw vegetables and the freedom to put something you like into your own oven. Others say going out to eat makes a night more fun, sociable and calming. Although all have their positive and bad points, Asians in the USA love a hot curry and enjoy it more when there is a choice to choose from. This is where restaurant cuisine comes in handy, as it offers various meals for all of you who want to eat. So if you are with your mates, you may select from a list and eat whatever you want, but if you are at home, let's just agree it is easier to consume everything.

However, food can always be roasted at restaurants to accommodate the crowd, rather than the person. Chicken Tikka Masala, for example, is a very common restaurant recipe, and maybe never named it in an Asian home when made. Personalized ingredients are used at home to create such a dish centered on relatives or previously acquired recipes. Ingredients like unique herbs, achaar, or yoghurt are used to create such a recipe that fits your own palate.

Asians enjoy the food but most especially eat it as quickly as possible on our tables. Eating in does not necessarily mean you are going to eat on time, since preparing Asian meals at home will take time utilizing established fresh produce and recipes. It is giving love and attention to your home, always cooking pays-off, particularly if it's something unique for someone!

You have a starter at restaurants, a main dish meal as well as a cake, but this is not that much for those of you with a huge appetite. You can feel like you do not get your money worth as the sizes of the section are rather limited. A Lamb Balti bowl, for instance, can cost around $6-8. If cooking at home, this quantity may suffice for you and your guests, with larger serving sizes and the opportunity, if needed, to incorporate more. All of us, Asians, are now victims to the fast-food community as Britain gets more urbanized. This is because of the hectic lives that we all live through. While most of the old people enjoy a good home-cooked dinner, the new ones consider it more convenient to eat out.

Chapter 02: Common Spices Used in Indian Cuisine and their Properties

Indian food includes the use of a large range of spices. They are mixed and used extensively in different recipes The same spice flavor may be rendered completely different with a slight change in the style of cooking. To discover these amazing products, we have identified several of India's most frequently used spices.

- **Red Powder Chili**

Red chili is produced of red chili seeds. It is extremely solid, being the strongest component of the chili, only used in limited amounts. The Americans and the Portuguese brought this substance to India, which has became an important part of Indian cuisine. Even the chili is used in numerous Southern Indian curries. The key feature of chili is hotness, probably due to its capsaicin portion, but there are types that also have a lot of fragrance and flavor.

- Mustard Seeds

Brown mustard seeds are more widely used in Indian cuisine than any other mustard seeds. These seeds may be roasted whole for flavoring oil which is then used for cooking raw food. Even this favourite oil may be used as a dipping sauce. Although the seeds are local in Rome, the closest approximation to their usage is in Buddha literature, where he uses certain seeds to save the life of a child.

- Coriander

Coriander is a part of the Parsley Genus, and when they mature, the seeds are round, ridged, and change its color from dark green to bright orange. This spice looks tangy and pleasant, with a mild citrusy aroma. This invisible spice is undoubtedly the world's oldest and is commonly cultivated in Rajasthan States.

- Cinnamon

Cinnamon is a sweet-flavored spice with a soft and woody fragrance. It is a perfect product for use in sweets and cakes. Cinnamon also has numerous benefits, including bringing spice to the food. Also it helps to reduce leukaemia and lower cholesterol. It is cultivated primarily along the Kerela and Tamil Nadu Western Ghats.

- Asafoetida

This is the cured resin emerging from a plant's base. It is particularly pungent in its natural state with a garlic like sulphur scent. However, the scent dies down when cooked in oil, and the flavour significantly improves.

Typically, asafoetida is added to boiling oil before some other component. It is prized for its truffle-like taste and roasted garlic scent and it is used in Indian food as a seasoning blend and flavoring agent. Asafoetida, grown primarily in Kashmir and some parts of Punjab. It is very beneficial for its bashing flatulence properties.

- Cumin

Cumin is extracted from the Parsley group and is used in most Indian sauces and veggies to give a smoky flavor and a strong fragrance. Cumin seeds are fried in its dry shape and cooked before use. It is typically the very first spice to be added while preparing Indian foods. It is often roasted dry and reduced to dust before adding to dishes such as pancakes and heavy cream. It is also used for flavoring meat, stuffed onions and tonnes of Indian cooking. It is used carefully since it burns quickly and may become intoxicating.

- Saffron

Saffron is the world's costly spice. Actually originated in Kashmir and originating from the prejudice of Cocus Bulbs. It is considered that saffron is more precious than money. Its most notable thing is its musky, honey-like scent. It is commonly used after soaking in water or milk, which eases its intense fragrance and taste.

- Tumeric

Another spice that belongs to the ginger tribe is tumeric. It is possibly the spice used mostly in India. Turmeric has been used primarily as a pigment, and for hundreds of years in traditional Ayurvedic. Generated from the roots of the Indian born leafy plant Curcuma Longa. It has an oaky quality and mild smell and flavour. It is used in items intended for cooking and skincare products. It has a wide variety of medical applications. It aids in coping with skin issues. Its powder could be used to heal open wounds. It also allows to deal with diabetes.

- Cardamom

It is the world's third most costly spice, primarily since it needs a lot of physical work. While it has a moderate and soft eucalyptus colour on the green cardamom, the black cardamom is coarse, smoky and usually mostly used for its seeds. The most popular usage for cardamom is to improve tea and pudding taste.

It is used to provide a strong taste and scent in most Indian and other sweet dishes. It is commonly used in the drug industry . It helps protect against poor smell and stomach disease. Whole chewed cardamom is ideal for dealing with diabetes.

- Indian Bay Leaf

Indian Bay Leaf is quite distinct from European Bay Leaf even though both belong to the Lauraceae tribe. They are the leaves of a cinnamon tree parent and are distinctive from their white shelves streaks that extend through the root. They are extremely light but have a heavy spice taste.

It grows in northern India, Himalayan slopes and Nepal. Sikkim State is the biggest producer in India, but it is most frequently formed from raw or wild plants. It is a critical element in Mughal food and produced in popular dishes like Korma and biryani.

- Ginger

Ginger is one of India's most valuable crops, with more than one thousand tonnes growth per year. Mostly the fresh ginger is used. Dry ginger is used only in certain states in India, such as Goa and Kashmir.

There are two major ginger types, called after the port they were transported from "Cochin" in the south of Kerala, and "Calicut" in the north of Kerala. Both are strongly aromatic with about 4 percent essential oil content and low fibre content. Owing to its milder and more nuanced taste, it is found to be superior to ginger grown in many other countries. Dried ginger is not as common as fresh ginger in Indian dishes.

- Leaves Curry

The curry leaves, which have little to do with spice, are the leaf of a bush in the Rutaceae family, which is local to India and Sri Lanka. This vegetation is very smelly and friendly. The curry tree is now cultivated in all parts of India but it is more cultivated in the Southern India. So many households have a plant in their greenhouse because it is simple to cultivate. The leaves are often used in the north (for example combined with potato and peas samosa stuffing). They are used in sauces of beef and poultry.

- Kalonji / Nigella

This plant has black triangular seeds, sometimes mistakenly referred to as black cumin, have a mild and somewhat bitter taste, with earthy tones and an onion-like pungent flavour. India is the leading supplier of Kalonji. Egypt and Morocco are the other production countries.

These seeds are also a potent antioxidant and are associated with several medicinal effects, against asthma, fever, pneumonia and other fall diseases.

- Ajowan

Another seed spice from a member of the family Umbelliferae is Ajowan. It has a faint bitter earthy flavour, and a fragrance identical to thyme but more strong. The process of cooking (especially baking) smooths the tendency to influence Ajowan, thus producing a rather peculiar nutty taste.

Rajasthan is India's leading Ajowan manufacturer, responsible for 90 percent of total production. Sometimes used for savoury snacks and baked goods in Indian cuisine, it gives a savoury feel to many vegetable meals. Its therapeutic properties vary from assisting with digestion to curing colds and eliminating bloating.

- Dark Brown Mustard

It is one of the few seasonings that is as popular in the states having the most flavor consuming nations such as Indonesia and India. In Europe and America, mustard seeds are almost solely used for producing the sauce of the very same name originating from the Roman mixture of mustard seeds with their distinctive sourness.

There are three mustard types that are the light, the brown and the black. The light one is the gentler, whereas the other two are pungent. It is also part of the North-East traditional spice blend. In this area, there is an Indian variant of mustard sauce produced from a mixture of mustard seeds that are soaked for a few days.

Mustard seeds only produce their pungency when grounded or compressed and combined with a fluid using the sourness and stabilise it with an acidic fluid.

- Fenugreek

Fenugreek is a herb of the Legumes family. Its plants are used in fresh, dry, and seed forms. The Hindi word is Methi. Its flavour is whacky and sour (toasting the seeds decreases the bitterness) and its usage is as common as a medicinal treatment in the kitchen. The seeds as a spice are mainly used in India, Turkey, but India is the main source and purchaser of it.

It is an essential component of curry in the kitchen. In Punjab, it is used to complement the flavour of vegetables such as pumpkin, and in the Southern India it is applied to dosa. Batter-dosa includes tasty Indian rice and dal pancakes (split lentils). It is also a component of the Bengali five-spice blend.

According to conventional medicine, it improves absorption and decreases the amount of sugar. It is often used to manage colitis and is recommended for mothers who are breastfeeding since it has a material that enhances the supply of milk.

- Clove

This tasty spice is the crisped unlabeled bud of a Myrtle family vine, indigenous to the island chains of Moluccas. The production of cloves extended beyond the Moluccas only towards the end of the XVIII century and the dominance was established. Now mostly in Indonesia, as well as in Tanzania, clove is still produced. South India production began in 1800 but mostly the clove now eaten is transported from Sri Lanka. The usage of clove in Indian cooking is restricted to mixes and masala. It is very high in fragrance and flavour. It is also used in many rice dishes.

Clove has one of the largest proportion of volatile oil relative to other spices, and a tiny quantity goes a long way for this. Clove is also the seasoning with the strongest antioxidant potential.

- Black Pepper

Pepper is the spice produced from the Piper nigrum plant berries. We do have three most popular varieties of pepper as per the period of harvest and the post-harvest process: white pepper, black pepper and green pepper.

In India, it is native in the southern area of Malabar and now Black Pepper also grows in Kerala, which is obtained by extracting the green drupes only as they are ripe and begin to turn red, and then by processing them under the sunlight or in a furnace until the humidity content is below a certain level. A process of oxidation occurs during the drying period. Black pepper can be used in many spice mixtures, meat and chicken dishes in the north.

- **Amchur Powder**

This is a sweet and malty spice which acts as a thickening agent and it is used as a dipping sauce. It gives a sour fruity taste to curries, sauces and chutneys.

Chapter 3: Indian Breakfast Recipes

The Indian Breakfast Recipes can be cooked in less time and can be useful for every one of you. Both Northern India breakfast dishes and Southern India breakfast dishes which can be cooked in a matter of minutes, are scattered throughout this chapter. Look at these Indian Recipes for the breakfast and brunch. You will now make them at home in the mornings easily by following given recipes.

Vegetable RavaUpma

Cooking time: 20 minutes
Serving meals: 2

- Ingredients

- 1 cup of Rava
- 1 sliced onion
- ¼ cup peas
- 1 cup of combined, diced vegetables
- 3 green, sliced chilies
- 1 tablespoon of ginger, sliced
- Just a couple leaves of curry
- ½ teaspoon urad dal
- ¼ teaspoon of mustard seeds
- Leaves of coriander, sliced, to marinade
- Oil 1 tablespoon
- Salt as per your liking

▢ Method

1) Take a big saucepan and add vegetable oil and heat it over medium-high heat.

2) Add all seeds that are finely chopped, red chilies and ginger. With a wooden skewer, blend the products together properly.

3) In a pan, add peas and dal in order to combine the products properly, flip the pan tightly.

4) Stir fry for a few moments then add curry leaves. Meanwhile, grab a cutting board and individually cut all the vegetables. Now in the pan put chopped vegetables and mix it all well.

5) Add ample water to the pan and sprinkle very well salt. Use a lid to cover the pan and cook it over medium-high heat.

6) Cook until a deep mixture is created. Now, for a couple of minutes, take a non-stick pan and add 1 tablespoon of oil and cook semolina in it over medium-high heat.

7) When vegetables are fried, add cooked semolina in small amount steadily, stirring constantly. Keep continuously stirring, and check that no chunks are created.

8) Cook on a low flame for 5 minutes and then move it to a serving bowl. Garnish it with cashews and mint leaves.

9) Serve immediately.

UpmaSooji with Coconut

Cooking time: 30 minutes
Servings: 4 persons

- Ingredients

- 1 cup sooji (semolina)
- 2 teaspoons of ghee
- 1 ½ teaspoon mustard seed
- Asafetida as much you like
- 10 split organic cashews
- 1 teaspoon of Chana dal and urad dal immersed in a bath at least for 10 minutes.
- 1 diced ginger tablespoon
- 1 tiny sliced red onion
- 1 diced green chili
- 10 leaves of curry
- 4 tablespoons of green peas
- 2.5 cups of water
- Salt as much you like
- 2 teaspoons of cilantro minced
- 1 teaspoon of ghee

- Method

1) Roast the sooji over a moderate flame until moist, continue to stir for around 5 minute. Take sooji off the pan and move it to some other dish.

2) This phase of frying sooji can be completed before and you can save time for packed mornings.

3) Now add two tablespoons of oil at medium heat to the same pan.

4) Then add seeds, hing, cashews, dal ginger and stir fry for 1 minute before they begin to change color.

5) Add carrot, green chili pepper and curry leaves. Once the onions are added, cook for an additional minute.

6) Then after sometime add the peas and stir. Heat till the fresh scent of peas falls out.

7) Add 3 cups of water. Then squeezed lemon zest into it and add cilantro and then, blend properly. If you want a little sweetness in your Upma, you can also add honey or sugar.

8) Put the water in it to a boil now. Until the water has boiled, start adding the cooked sooji little by little at the moment.

9) With a dough scraper, blend sooji in one way after each inclusion.

10) Then cover it with a lid over the pot and adjust heat to normal. Let it stay this way for some time.

11) Remove the cover and add ghee 2 teaspoon. That is voluntary, but it is encouraged. Switch the heat off.

12) Upma is served warm with coconut chutney.

Puffed Upma Rice

Serving to 1–2 persons

Cooking time: 15 minutes

Ingredients

- 3 puffed rice cups
- 1 tiny onion
- 1 tiny tomato
- 1-2 chilies
- ½ teaspoon powder of turmeric
- Seeds with ½ teaspoon mustard
- 1 sliced dry red chili
- Just a couple leaves of curry
- 2 teaspoon of oil
- Salt as per your liking

Methods

1) Chop everything.
2) Heat a skillet with one tablespoon of oil. Add seeds in it.
3) Insert dry red chili and urad dal in the frying seeds. Fry until dal turns into brown color.
4) And add all chopped stuff in it.
5) Also, salt as per your liking and turmeric in it.
6) Cover for a minute and let it cook for a while.
7) Take the puffed rice and add running water via the puffed rice to literally wash it. Try squeezing the water out and quickly return it to the plate.
8) Add it in a pan. And cook over high heat for a moment.
9) Remove it from the heat.
10) Immediately serve puffed Upma rice.

Things to be Noted

- Do not wash the puffed rice in water, as it gets soggy.

- Upma-puffed rice is better eaten when wet.

Tamarind and RavaUpma Rice

Cooking time: 20-30 min
Serves 6-8 people

- Ingredients

  - 2 cups Rava rice
  - 1 onion thinly chopped
  - 3-4 green chili with a cut
  - ½ roughly chopped ginger
  - 1 cup of minced vegetables
  - 1 ½ teaspoons ghee
  - 9 cashew-nuts (optional)
  - 4 cups of water
- Salt

For Seasoning Purposes:

- 1 teaspoon of mustard seeds
- 1 curry sprig leaves
- 1 teaspoon seeds of cumin
- 1 teaspoon gram of Bengal
- 1 teaspoon black dal

- Method

1) *In a pan, heat the oil, add cumin and seeds in it.*

2) Insert curry leaves, onion and green chilies and then let the color change with the leaves.

3) Add the dal in it and fry until the dal is finely baked in oil.

4) Add water in it and let it to boil. Put salt as per your liking.

5) Add rice rava constantly when cooking.

6) Stir well, cover the lid and cook over medium-high heat until all of the humidity is consumed.

7) Lower the flame and steam until they are cooked.

8) Turn the heat off and serve it.

RagiRavaIdli

It helps to protect the integrity of the bones and avoids osteoporosis for those with low haemoglobin concentrations. It is a decent source of natural fiber and is gluten free as well. Ragiidli is a really nutritious meal which is ideal for children and the elderly. These idlis are soft, healthy and spongy.

Servings: 4 persons

- Ingredients

- Idli rice 1 cup
- Flour 2 cups
- 1 cup dal
- ½ teaspoon seeds of fenugreek

- Salt if required

▣ Steps to Follow

1) Wash and soak seeds, urad dal and fenugreek for 4 hours. For 5 hours, clean and rinse the rice independently.
2) Crush dal and seeds until it become sleek and creamy. Remove in a container, and set it aside.
3) Crush the rice to make it flour and add water in it to prepare a visibly rough mixture or batter.
4) Now add rice batter into a dal seeds mixture. Add salt and other spices all together until combined properly.
5) The strength of the batter should be close to the Idli batter.
6) Take the wet blender out of it and blend really well with your fingertips.
7) Allow it to settle for some time. To keep it from spilling, use a wide vessel since it can double during fermentation.
8) Our batter RagiIdli is set.

▣ How to Cook RagiIdli

1) Hot the water in an idle or steamer vessel. Mix well the soaked ragiidli batter and pour a spoonful of idli batter in the oiled moulds and put it into the broiler pan.
2) Heat to cook for 20 minutes or a toothpick placed in the idli core comes out clean.
3) After 5 minutes, extract it from the mould using a teaspoon submerged in water.
4) Serve the hot RagiIdli with your option of chutney.

RavaIdliSabbakki

Cook Time: 12 minutes
Servings: 15

Ingredients

- 1 Sooji cup
- 1 tablespoon mustard seeds
- Cumin seeds with one teaspoon
- 1 tablespoon Chana dal
- 1 tablespoon Black Dal (Split)
- Cashew nuts 1/3 cup, sliced
- 1 sprig of shredded curry leaves
- Ginger 1 tablespoon
- Asafoetida as per your liking
- 2 chilies, chopped
- Oil as per your use
- 2 tablespoons of coriander thinly sliced
- Salt
  - ¼ cup Tapioca Perls
  - 1 cup Curd, battered
  - Oil for greasing

Method

1) Firstly, simmer tapioca perls in enough water for two hours. Filter this and squeeze out the extra water using your fingertips, do not panic if it partially crumbles or loses its form.

2) In a moderate-flame pan, heat oil. Add seeds and let it vibrate. After some time add cumin seeds and dal mixture. Mix in a low flame until it becomes golden

3) Add hinges, curry, ginger and chilies at this point and cook for 5 minutes, ensure that the products are cooked perfectly.

4) This helps the Ravaidli mix to be processed for potential usage in an airtight bag. Add the Rava and roast, then switch off the flame after 5 minutes.

5) Heat water in idli steamer. Lubricate the moulds of Idli.

6) Add Ravaidli mixture, strained tapioca perls, coriander leaves, salt as per your liking and yoghurt in a bowl and mix and give it a nice blend.

7) Change the batter's reliability to a thick consistency.

8) Force the batter into the idlimould and heat for 15 minutes.

9) Sprinkle with some oil and serve it.

Ravaldli: Foxtail Millet

Cooking time: 10 minutes
Servings: 3

▪ Ingredients

- Millet Foxtail-3 cups
- Dal: 1 cup
- Fenugreek Seed – ¼ tablespoon
- Oil as required
- Water as required
- Salt as per your liking

▪ Method

1) Clean and simmer the millet and Urad Dal in different bowl of water for 6 hours. Along with the Dal, you can immerse Fenugreek seeds in water.

2) Crush your millet and Dal individually.

3) Move the soaked dal and Fenugreek beans in a processor and grind them to a fine paste. Drop it into a bowl. Next, grind the submerged millet in the same blender. Shift it and the Dal batter to the bowl.

4) Balance well the batter and all that for overnight to ferment. Mix well after fermenting.

5) Add salt and blend properly before frying. Add the necessary water to the batter to prepare Idli and get to the consistency of the idli batter. Lubricate the idli plate with butter, then steam for 10 mins in medium-low heat.

6) Enable it to cool down a bit, then sprinkle with little water and extract the hot Idli.

7) Add water to prepare the dosa and change the batter to the consistency required. Heat a dosatawa and pour a spoonful of batter and distribute evenly. Cook and sprinkle oil around the rim.

8) Flip the other side and fry and then serve it.

DosaRava Onion

Cooking time: 15 minutes
Servings to 3 persons

Ingredients

- Half cup of semolina (sooji)
- 2 teaspoons sliced coriander

- 1 sprig Stripped curry
- Half cup flour of rice
- 1 tablespoon roughly minced ginger
- 1 sliced chili
- ¼ cup of Maida
- One teaspoon cumin seeds
- 1 thinly sliced onion
- Ghee-where appropriate

◾ Method

1) Get all of the products in a cup except onions and add water. For fast mixing use a whisker.
2) Hold aside the onions. The batter must be really thin.
3) Preferably, heat a non-stick dosa plate. It should be heated. Drizzle and spill the soupy batter with some grease, first making a larger ring and then filling in the middle.
4) Instantly scatter over the sliced onions on it. Add a teaspoon of oil/ghee to it. Let the moderate flame cook till the dosa turns to a golden hue.
5) Then serve it.

Dosa Buckwheat

It is simple to prepare this nutritious and safe dosa and it is a perfect replacement for bread. Buckwheat has a robust and mildly nutty taste that goes well with a number of fillings. This recipe allows the batter to rest for at least overnight to enable the flours to be mixed with water. We schedule this and make it stand over time so that the next day it is able to be used. The batter can be kept for up to 2 days in the fridge.

Servings: 10 persons
Cooking time: 10 min

🔖 Ingredients

- 1 cup of flour for Buckwheat
- ½ cup Oat flour
- ½ cup almond flour
- Water as your liking
- ½ tsp of salt

🔖 Method

1) To prepare a softer batter: whisk Buckwheat, oat, and salted almond flours. Cover and allow to remain in the refrigerator at room temperature for at overnight.
2) Add water and mix it well.
3) Set a temperature for Dosa maker machine to setting 1.
4) To the upper and bottom cooking racks, grease it with a thin layer of oil. Pour spoonful of batter in.
5) Cook for 3 minutes. Open to inspect the dosa, and cook for 1 minute if necessary.
6) Serve it.

DosaDhaniaPalak

Cooking Time 10 min
For 5 Individuals

🔖 Ingredients

- 2 ½ cups rice, has to be soaked overnight
- 1 cup Dal, has to be soaked overnight
- One tablespoon Fenugreek Seeds
- Salt as per your liking
- Leaves of Spinach and Coriander, finely sliced
- Oil to use

Method

1) For the preparation of dosa, wash the rice, spinach and coriander in water. Let the rice completely submerged in water. Let it simmer for about six hours.

2) Drench the dal and fenugreek in water, so that the whole dal is fully submerged in water. Let them simmer for about six hours.

3) When saturated, grind the dal into a fluffy batter. Only add sufficient water when grinding to turn it into a really softer batter. The batter is going to appear fluffy. Put this batter into a bowl.

4) Crush the rice into a somewhat smooth batter, add only the amount of water needed to process. Using a lot of water would make it too watery for the dosa mixture. The rice batter can be a little bit softer, but it must be extremely soft for the dal batter.

5) Merge the dal and the rice batter, add salt as per your liking and settle it down for the batter fermentation process for at least overnight. You will note that the amount of the batter will have gone up. That is why you can position the batter in a wide jar.

6) In a blender grinder, blend spinach leaves and coriander to create a perfect paste and hold aside.

7) Stir rapidly with a spatula until the batter gets its thickness, and add the salt as per the flavor.

8) Now add the paste and combine the vegetable mixture, so that all is well absorbed.

9) Steam a dosa, and apply a few drops of oil. Lubricate the tawa(pan) with a limited quantity of oil.

10) Take a batter handful and drop back down in the tawa middle. Spread it uniformly in a clockwise direction into the outside.

11) Apply a few drops of oil from the edges and even in the middle. Fry the dosa till it gets brown at the bottom. And then serve it.

DosaAval

Cooking time: 20 mins
Servings to 4 persons

🔹 Ingredients

- 3 cups of rice
- 1 cup dal
- 2 tsp fenugreek seeds
- Salt
- Ghee or oil, as per your liking
- Water according to requirements

🔹 Method

1) Rinse rice in the water and dal in running water individually, and simmer it in containers with just enough salted water.

2) Let the rice and dal simmer in the bath for a minimum of 6 hours before overnight.

3) Wash aval and add it to the washed rice bowl with water.

4) Grind the dal, rice mixture and fenugreek seeds in a grinder until it becomes smooth batter.

5) Set the oven for 15 minutes to 180 degrees and then switch it off.
6) Hold the overnight batter in an oven.
7) Add salt in the batter the next day.
8) Heat a DosaTawa and pour a ladle of dosa batter.
9) Range uniformly with the aid of a slotted spoon. Sprinkle the sides with some oil.
10) Cook until it turns out to be golden.

DadpePohe

Servings to 3 persons
Cooking time 30 minutes

☐ Ingredients

- 1 ½ cups Small Flattened Rice
- 1 cup of onion thinly Sliced
- ¾ Cup coconut grated
- Powdered Sugar 2 tablespoon
- Lemon zest 2-3 teaspoons
- Fresh Peanuts 3 teaspoons
- Two tablespoon Leaves of Coriander
- Salt as per your liking or taste
- Oil 3 teaspoons
- Asafetida ¼ teaspoon

☐ Method

1) Mix the finely sliced onions, coconut grated, cinnamon, sugar and lemon zest.

2) Scatter smooth flattened rice in a bowl and mix at the rim.

3) Heat a pan and add cooking oil to it. Insert the fresh peanuts and fried before they shift hue. Remove and set aside.

4) Now add the mustard seeds to the same hot oil and add the asafetida, chopped chilies and leaves of curry. Turn off the flame and add the turmeric powder. Mix it well.

5) Put this mixture over the ready pohe.

6) Offer a quick flip of the whole mix.

7) Shield and hold aside for around 10 to 15 minutes to merge and relax all the tastes.

8) Serve this tasty DadpaePohe for brunch or snack at any time.

Pohe Tomato with Peas

Cooking time: 50 mins
Serving to 3 persons

❓   Ingredients

- Two teaspoons of olive oil
- 1 Big, minced onion
- 1 Clove of garlic, thinly minced
- 3 Small-sized tomatoes, thinly sliced
- ½ cup of sugar
- One spoonful of new oregano
- 1 of a cup of water or as you required
- One teaspoon of tomato
- 1 Small diced zucchini,
- 1 cup of peas
- Salt

▪ Method

1) Refresh to fill poha with only enough water and keep away for 10 minutes.
2) After 10 minutes, absolutely drain the water, release the poha and separate the lumps, if any.
3) Add salt, turmeric powder, lime zest and red chili powder in it.
4) Use a ladle and blend properly.
5) Heat oil in a large frying pan or large base pan.
6) Add the seeds of mustard and cumin.
7) Let them split.
8) Stir-fry light brown on medium-low flame before the onions transform. Add the vegetables and combine well.
9) After some time add the nuts and poha. Cook it for 5 minutes and blend properly.
10) Move to a bowl for serving.
11) Garnish it with coriander and serve right away.

Rotli'sVaghareli

Serving to 2 persons
Cooking time: 30 minutes

▪ Ingredients

- 4 or 5 chapattis left over
- One cup of yoghurt-a good chance to use the extra natural yoghurt in the refrigerator.
- 2 teaspoons of garlic
- 1 spoonful of mustard seeds.
- Two smashed green chilies

- 1 tablespoon of turmeric
- 1 spoonful of cooking oil
- Salt with flavor
- A tiny collection of cilantro
- One lemon tablespoon

▶ Method

1) Break the chappatis into bits.

2) In a saucepan heat the oil. Add the seeds and switch the heat to medium.

3) Add bits of chappati and swirl them in oil.

4) Mix the mustard, turmeric, garlic, chilies in it.

5) Add a cup and a half of water and yoghurt in it and also mix it well.

6) Add the chapattis to this and let it cook in normal heat.

7) Allow the mixture to cook for 5 minutes, then include sugar and lemon in it.

8) To the mixture, add coriander and stir well. They will soak up the liquids while the chapattis cook. If the mixture begins to cling to the bottom of the saucepan, you may need to add more hot water.

9) With a touch of sweet and sour, the flavor of this dish should be mild, so change the taste to your preference. Serve it.

- Bengali Vegetable Form Pohe

Cooking time: 40 minutes

▪ Ingredients

For batter you need:
- Maida ½ cup
- ½ semolina cup (sooji)
- 1 tablespoon of sugar
- 1 tablespoon of shredded fennel seeds
- Evaporated milk 350ml
- Oil as per you needs for frying.

For sugar syrup you need:
- 1 Cup of drinking water
- Four green cardamom
- 1 cup of sugar

▪ Method

1) Get all the items specified for a batter in a medium bowl and blend them properly, so that no chunks are there. Add just a little milk if you like it is too dense. Let it rest for some time.

2) Put the ingredients for sugar sauce in a saucepan and cook them together until you have syrup of one string.

3) Hot enough oil in a pan to deep fry.

4) To shape a tiny pancake of 2 diameters, pour a spoon of flour in the liquid.

5) Fry on medium fire. Cook and turn one side over.

6) Suppose all sides turn brown remove with a spatula and indulge in sugar syrup instantly. Leave for 1 minute to full.

7) Remove hot, and serve it.

The Sesame and Beetroot Thepla

Cooking Time: 25 min
Serving to 2 persons

Ingredients
- 1 Grated Beetroot
- ½ cup of Ground wheat
- ½ cup of besan
- ½ teaspoon cumin powder
- ½ Amchur teaspoon
- ½ teaspoon powder of Garam masala
- 1 teaspoon mixture of Red Chili
- Oil as per you need
- Salt as per your taste

Directions

1) Add all the herbs, salt and ghee with the diced beetroot.
2) Also add wheat and besan flour and squeeze a soft mixture with water.
3) Take a small portion and shape it into a thepla.
4) Heat up the Tawa and put a thepla on it.
5) Heat it for about a minutes and then turn it and heat about a minute but at the other side.
6) Serve it with curd.

Dhokla Buckwheat Corn

Servings to 5 persons
Cooking time: 35 minutes

Ingredients

- Two minced Green Chilies
- Chopped 1 Ginger
- ½ teaspoon soda for frying
- 2 teaspoon of fruit salt
- ½ teaspoon Turmeric powder
- 2 tablespoons Sunflower Oil
- 1/3 cup of Water
- 2 cups Gram (besan) flour
- 1 cup water, or more where possible
- 2 teaspoons of salt to taste

Method

1) Start preparing all the items to start cooking the Dhokla.
2) Grease and leave aside a cake tray or a dhokla plate. Get a steamer prepared with water and have it loaded.
3) Next, create a combination of chili and ginger. Add this combination and water into a shallow blender mixer jar and combine to create a puree. Hold this away.
4) Put all the items along with the above paste into a large bowl and hold aside.
5) Whisk well to mix, add lemon zest and soda will froth up the Dhokla batter.
6) Into the lubricated plate, put the Dhokla batter and put it in the steamer ready.
7) Wrap the steamer and switch the heat on and steam it for 15 minutes.
8) If you stick a knife in the middle and along the sides and it falls out dry, you will recognize when it is finished.

9) Remove from the steamer the KhamanDhokla, and leave it to cool fully.

The next move is to prepare the water in the sugar lemon:

10) Heat a skillet over medium heat with oil. Add the mustard seeds and cumin seeds, and let it crack. Apply the green chilies and curry leaves and mix for about a minute until it crackles.

11) If done, add the water, lemon zest, salt and sugar. Remove it before the sugar dissolves, then switch off the fire. Let the tadka cool off a little.

12) From over KhamanDhokla, sponge the tadka so that it gets well saturated.

13) Remove it from the pan and serve it.

Conclusion

Indian food can be both thrilling and daunting, with all its exotic products, unfamiliar sauces, and tongue-tingling tastes. It is a complete world of taste. To get a titillating culinary experience, you mix many of the strategies from other cuisines and incorporate mysterious spices. Do not be afraid to start cooking Indian food at home. First, the different dishes and flavors that make up Indian food are important to consider. The food in India is as popular as you can find in Europe. All are entirely new, and the only element that links is a judicious awareness of the usage of spices.

There are 20 to 30 essential spices used in many sauces, such as cumin, coriander, turmeric, and ginger, to name a handful, and there are numerous ways to use them. Spices have cardiovascular advantages, and they also make the meal more tasty and entertaining.

In history, geography and environment, variety can be seen in India's cuisine. Spices are a crucial part of the preparation of food and are used to increase a dish's taste. For the proper preparation of Indian cuisine, accurate usage and combining of the aromatic spices are essential. Also, oil is an essential part of cooking, be it mustard oil in the north or coconut oil in the south. Vegetables differ according to season and area. The vegetables are cooked as a main dish.

Indian Food has an extra advantage for vegetarians. It is one of the most comfortable cuisines around for them. Judicious application of seasoning and sauces bring the taste of potatoes, cauliflower, spinach, and eggplant. Keep things easy at home as you start out.

www.ingramcontent.com/pod-product-compliance
Lightning Source LLC
Chambersburg PA
CBHW071829080526
44589CB00012B/958